THE
NONFICTION
BOOK
PUBLISHING PLAN

*THE PROFESSIONAL GUIDE TO
PROFITABLE SELF-PUBLISHING*

**STEPHANIE CHANDLER
KARL W. PALACHUK**

The Nonfiction Book Publishing Plan
The Professional Guide to Profitable Self-Publishing
By Stephanie Chandler and Karl W. Palachuk
1. LAN027000 2. LAN002000 3. REF026000
Print ISBN: 978-1-949642-00-1
Ebook ISBN: 978-1-949642-01-8
Printed in the United States of America

Authority Publishing
11230 Gold Express Dr. #310-413
Gold River, CA 95670
800-877-1097
AuthorityPublishing.com

 # CONTENTS

Want to connect with fellow authors?

You'll find your tribe, and a whole bunch of membership benefits, via the Nonfiction Authors Association!

www.NonfictionAuthorsAssociation.com

CHAPTER 1
THE BUSINESS OF SELF-PUBLISHING NONFICTION BOOKS

You may be wondering why this book is geared toward nonfiction authors. Isn't the publishing process the same no matter the genre? Yes and no.

While many of the processes for producing a book are the same regardless of genre, it's the *strategy* behind nonfiction that makes a big difference. Many nonfiction authors have a personal mission to make some kind of difference in the world, and just as many want to use their books as the basis for starting a business or as a way to grow an existing business. If you aren't yet thinking this way, you should be.

Publishing a book makes you an entrepreneur, and therefore you should treat your book like a business. Owning a business has many advantages. You can write off business expenses, such as the fees you pay to freelancers who help produce your book. If you have a home office, you may even be able to write off part of your utilities (talk to a qualified tax professional to find out exactly what you can and can't do).

The point is that we want you to treat your book like a business, not only because of the tax advantages, but because we want you to make money doing what you love. With more than one million books published each year, it's easier than ever to get a book in print. At the same time, many would argue that it's also harder to sell books and actually become profitable. You have to rise above the noise to stand out.

If you focus on book sales alone, and you earn somewhere between $5 and $15 per book as a self-published author, you have to sell a whole lot of books to pay your mortgage. It can be done, but the reality is that it won't be easy.

Our perspective is that authors should think beyond the book and use it as a tool to grow a business. This is exactly what we've both done, and we want to show you how you can do the same.

OPPORTUNITIES IN NONFICTION

Nielsen BookScan tracks around 85% of all print book sales in the U.S., and for 2017, it reported that over 687 million books were sold. When the ebook market exploded and we all feared that print books were going the way of vinyl records, the book market looked grim. But the decline in print book sales leveled out in 2013, and overall print book sales have increased every year since then.

Adult trade nonfiction became the fastest growing trade category of book sales in 2013, surpassing children/young adult, which had been the growth leader for the previous two years. Adult nonfiction also showed the strongest year-over-year growth among the five trade-sector subcategories tracked (the others: adult fiction, juvenile fiction, juvenile nonfiction, religion).

Sales in the adult nonfiction category have continued to increase each year, though numbers have leveled out. In 2017, the category gained 3% in sales over the previous year, while fiction declined by 1%.

What you might find even more interesting is that **nonfiction titles sell more than twice the number of fiction titles each**

year. In 2017, Nielsen BookScan reported 281 million adult nonfiction book sales compared to 139 million adult fiction titles sold. Juvenile nonfiction was up almost 8% over the previous year with nearly 60 million units sold, though fiction still leads with kids at 181 million units.

Incidentally, juvenile nonfiction sales have been increasing in recent years, which may be partly due to the Common Core standards used by many schools across the nation. Most teachers are encouraging their students to read 50% fiction and 50% nonfiction, with the goal of preparing students for a more successful college experience.

In more good news for nonfiction authors, an annual survey conducted by Smashwords revealed that nonfiction readers are far less price sensitive than fiction readers. Smashwords encourages nonfiction authors to experiment with higher ebook prices versus the lower ebook prices fiction writers must offer based on market demand (for fiction, Smashwords currently indicates $2.99 and $3.99 as the "sweet spots" for pricing).

The massive sales of nonfiction prove that there are growing opportunities in this category. It also makes us wonder why more writers' conferences and writers' groups aren't paying attention to nonfiction.

MORE REASONS TO LOVE NONFICTION

What do the following books have in common?

- *What to Expect When You're Expecting* by Heidi Murkoff and Sharon Mazel
- *Tuesdays with Morrie* by Mitch Albom
- *The Purpose-Driven Life* by Rick Warren
- *The 7 Habits of Highly Effective People* by Stephen R. Covey
- *Men Are from Mars, Women Are from Venus* by John Gray
- *Eat, Pray, Love* by Elizabeth Gilbert

- *A New Earth* by Eckhart Tolle
- *The Four Agreements* by Don Miguel Ruiz
- *Chicken Soup for the Soul* by Jack Canfield and Mark Victor Hansen
- *Good to Great* by Jim Collins
- *A Child Called It* by Dave Pelzer
- *The Last Lecture* by Randy Pausch
- *Into the Wild* by Jon Krakauer
- *The Tipping Point* by Malcolm Gladwell
- *The Audacity of Hope* by Barack Obama
- *Running with Scissors* by Augusten Burroughs
- *The Glass Castle* by Jeannette Walls
- *He's Just Not That into You* by Greg Behrendt, Liz Tuccillo
- *Dr. Atkins New Diet Revolution* by Robert C. Atkins
- *The South Beach Diet* by Arthur Agatston

All of these nonfiction books topped bestseller lists in the last twenty years, and they are all titles that continue to sell well today. Some were turned into movies or featured on Oprah. All have contributed to incredibly successful careers for the authors who wrote them.

The point is that nonfiction can be evergreen. It can stay relevant for many, many years. Remember *How to Win Friends and Influence People* by Dale Carnegie? It was originally published in 1936 and has sold over 30 million copies. As recently as 2011, this book was listed in *Time* magazine's list of *The 100 Most Influential Books of All Time*. It continues to appear on recommended reading lists around the world and still sells swiftly today.

Nonfiction books can generate revenues for years, and even for decades. But let's be clear: only a small percentage of authors will ever make a living from their books alone. Even most *New York Times* bestselling authors have day jobs. They also earn money from speaking, consulting, writing columns for major publications, teaching classes, and building other revenue streams. Often a book is the first step in building a highly profitable business.

AUTHOR PERSPECTIVE: *Karl Palachuk*

I run two businesses in Sacramento, California. One is a technology consulting company. The other is a book publishing company, which grew out of my activities publishing almost two dozen books for myself and others.

I have written seventeen books prior to this one. I self-published most of those and worked with another small company that self-published one. My first book was published way back in 2005 when digital printing was neither cheap nor widespread. Back in those dark ages, the only way to get a good price on book printing was to buy 1,000 copies at a time.

My first book cost about $8 to produce when printed in quantities of 1,000 at a time. In other words, I had to come up with $8,000 in order to get a garage full of books to sell. I had to *really* believe that I was going to be able to sell these books in order to commit to the printing!

As you'll see when we discuss pricing, however, I am very happy to be publishing in the nonfiction market. Why? Because I can charge a lot more for my books than I would ever get for a work of fiction.

I didn't need to sell 500 books to get my money back. In fact, that first book retailed for $90. So even with giveaways and promotions, I had to sell only 100 books to recoup my investment. And, as you can imagine, I had quite of bit of profit by the time the first 1,000 books were sold.

Because of my publications, I have been able to build my publishing career to include speaking at professional conferences, paid training events for major vendors, and a whole series of add-on and spin-off products. I have also developed an online store that is focused on my core market (technical consultants).

Let me be very clear on this point: It took a great deal of work to build up all of those spin-off products, training materials, websites, and so forth. It took time and money and hard work.

But let me also assure you that it is very realistic that you can build a little "empire" of your own around your books. It begins with your expertise and knowledge. Then it proceeds to your book, to speaking engagements, to additional work, and on from there.

AUTHOR PERSPECTIVE: *Stephanie Chandler*

Back in 2003, I quit my soul-sucking Silicon Valley job and opened a 2800-square-foot bookstore in Sacramento, California. My big master plan was to sit in the back office and write novels, because when you spend your whole life wanting to be a writer, crafting the Great American Novel seems to be the only logical thing to do. (Yes, I can laugh about it all now.)

As it turns out, I lacked the imagination to write fiction, and this realization was devastating, though only briefly. Luckily, I accidentally fell in love with nonfiction when I realized that I could write books that make a difference in the world.

Nonfiction books teach us how to do things and how to make life better. In addition to wanting to be a writer since I was a kid, I have always loved teaching. It was joyous to realize that I could blend two of my passions together and build a career around them.

My first book was a business startup guide that I self-published with the help of a hybrid publishing firm back in 2005. At the same time, I launched a website targeted toward entrepreneurs and started writing articles and building an audience. A year later, I wrote a second book, and because I had built a "platform" (an audience of book buyers) online, I quickly landed a book deal with Wiley. Then I signed with an agent and sold two more books. I eventually got turned off by traditional publishing and left it behind, then launched my own hybrid publishing company in 2008, specializing exclusively in nonfiction.

Being an author with an online platform helped me build a business I never expected. I was invited to speak at events and hired as a consultant. I ended up working with dozens of companies who paid sponsorship dollars in exchange for outreach to my audience. I was paid for writing posts on my own blog, posts on sponsors' blogs, recording video tips, conducting webinars and Twitter chats, and developing custom content. I even had a six-figure contract to serve as a spokesperson for a company, which involved doing a media tour, speaking at two events, conducting a couple of webinars, and writing some blog posts. And guess how that company found me? *They picked up a copy of one of my books.* I earned more from that one sponsorship agreement than I ever did from sales of that book.

Since then I have launched all kinds of revenue streams, from downloadable products to online training courses. In 2010, I launched the Nonfiction Writers Conference, an online event featuring 15 speakers over three days, all delivered via teleseminar. Each year attendees asked how they could keep in touch after the event was over, so in response I launched the Nonfiction Authors Association in 2013. Our community has grown beyond any of my wildest dreams, and it's also one of the most rewarding endeavors of my life.

What Karl and I hope to accomplish with this book is to help you think bigger about your publishing goals. It's not just about the book; it's about all the opportunities you can create around the book. And since many of us nonfiction authors want to make a difference in the world, it's also about how you can make your own dent in the universe along the way.

Karl and I have been in a mastermind group together for many years, and we have always wanted to collaborate on a project together. This book made perfect sense. My sincere hope is that we can inspire you to not only get your book published in the most professional way possible but to also build a rewarding and profitable business. Your book doesn't have to be a hobby. It can be the basis of a thriving business and the launch point for doing important work in the world.

ON MAKING A DENT IN THE UNIVERSE

Nonfiction books have the potential to change readers' lives. Want to learn how to sell on eBay? There's a book for that (many books, actually). Want to learn about the history of the state where you live? There is likely a book for that (and if there isn't, you should write one!). Want to become a master cupcake baker or learn how to ride a unicycle? Check your local library or bookstore.

What we want you to understand is that as an author, your book can impact your readers. Your book could teach readers how to improve their lives in some way, get healthier, grow a business, be a better parent, get through a challenging life event, manage menopause, care for an aging parent, live with an illness, become a better partner, get over a breakup, find new love, master the art of Origami, become a potato farmer, negotiate the purchase of your next car, and so much more.

Yes, being an author gives you the magical power to make a difference in the world!

And by the way, if you're writing a memoir, one of the first questions you should ask yourself is "What's in it for the reader?" Will readers relate to your journey in some way? Will they learn how to do something better because of your experience? Will they develop a deeper appreciation for their own family because of yours? Like prescriptive nonfiction, your memoir can—and should—impact readers' lives too.

The other challenge to keep in mind is that if you want to grow your readership and impact the world in some way, you have to help people find your book. With millions of competitors, it's easy for a book to get lost in the crowd. Like it or not, your job doesn't end when you write and publish the book. In many ways it's just beginning. We'll talk about this more in the coming pages.

CHAPTER 2
PROS AND CONS OF TRADITIONAL PUBLISHING AND SELF-PUBLISHING

Though this book is focused on how to self-publish your nonfiction book, we thought you should understand some of the pros and cons of both self-publishing and traditional publishing.

SELF-PUBLISHING PROS

- Book can get to market quickly—or on your own timeline.

- Full creative control of the cover art, interior design, and contents of your entire manuscript.

- Keep all of your rights. If you want to sell rights to a movie production company, have it translated into 59 languages, or publish excerpts in blogs and magazines, you can do so without getting permission or splitting the profits.

- Book printing costs are low, resulting in a higher profit margin when you sell books yourself.

- Distribution is readily available to Amazon and other online bookstores, making it easier than ever to reach readers, especially since the majority of us buy books online anyway.

- Print-on-demand technology means that you don't have the expense or headaches of printing and storing thousands of books in your garage or basement.

SELF-PUBLISHING CONS

- There is still some stigma in self-publishing, though it's improved in recent years.

- You have to do all the work: establish a publishing company, purchase ISBNs, get the cover created, get the interior typeset, get listed with distributors, locate a printer, etc.

- Startup costs can be high since you have to invest in editing and book-production services.

- It is difficult to get brick-and-mortar bookstore distribution, though not impossible (and not necessarily the best way to go anyway—we'll cover this more soon).

TRADITIONAL PUBLISHING PROS

- Some added credibility when your book is published with a major press.

- Broader distribution is more likely, including brick-and-mortar bookstores (though not guaranteed, and not necessarily the best choice for niche topics).

- Large media outlets are friendlier to traditionally published authors (more likely to get book reviews, major press coverage, etc.).

- Sometimes the publisher invests in marketing, though keep your expectations low. In most cases, publishers rely on the author to do the majority of the marketing. Large publishing houses tend to invest most of their resources into their well-known authors, though smaller and mid-sized publishers may put more effort into helping the book get exposure.

TRADITIONAL PUBLISHING CONS

- It typically takes a year or more for a traditional publisher to release a book.

- Unless you make it onto a major bestsellers list, you aren't likely to get rich. Publishers pay authors an average of $1 per book sold.

- Book advances are lower than ever, averaging around $5,000 to $10,000 for non-celebrities. And you must earn that back through book sales, $1 at a time, before you will see any additional royalties. Only a small percentage of authors ever earn back their book advance.

- The publisher has all the control. They can remove chapters from your manuscript, change your title, design a cover you don't like, etc. They can even decide to kill your project before it ever makes it to store shelves.

- You will lose the rights to your work. For example, most publishers require exclusive rights to sell the ebook version of your book, meaning that you can't sell or distribute your ebook version yourself. This also means you'll only receive a small portion of the ebook sales. The same can be true for audiobook rights, foreign book rights, and even screen rights.

There is also no harm in pursuing a traditional book deal if this is a personal goal for you. The process forces you to get clear about your marketing plans, your audience, and the overall mission for your book. If this is important to you, the biggest risk may be the time lost in the process of seeking agents and publishers. However, if too many doors close, you can always decide to self-publish later.

STEPHANIE'S PERSPECTIVE: *Why I Left Traditional Publishing in Favor of Self-Publishing*

Back in 2005, I had written my first manuscript for a business startup guide, and I attended a writer's conference where I had the opportunity to pitch agents. Many requested proposals, but in the months that followed, my mailbox filled with rejection letters. Thankfully, one of the agents—the wonderful Michael Larsen—took time to call me. He said, "I like what you're doing, but nobody knows who you are. You need to build a platform. You need to be out speaking to thousands of people each year."

This is what it all boils down to with nonfiction publishers: **Platform.** And for good reason. When you have a platform (which essentially means you have an established audience of potential book buyers), book sales are practically guaranteed. Publishers want to place their bets on authors who have the highest probability of generating sales.

After that fateful call, I decided I would begin building my platform online. I started blogging before blogging was a thing, and I noticed that the more content I added to my site, the more traffic the site received. I built a mailing list, began selling digital products, and before I knew it, I had an audience.

In the meantime, I decided to self-publish my first book, and it sold well, which showed me why publishers want authors with an audience. A year later I wrote my next manuscript and sent proposals to exactly two publishers. I signed a book deal within weeks—all thanks to the platform I had built.

NAVIGATING THE WORLD OF TRADITIONAL PUBLISHING

I learned a lot from that book deal. First, the contract was over twenty pages long, and it might as well have been written in a foreign language. I decided to hire a publishing expert to help me understand the terms and what I could and couldn't negotiate (such as my wholesale purchase price, turnaround time, and digital rights).

Overall, I had a pretty good experience with that first book. The editor didn't change a word in my manuscript, and though it typically takes most publishers a year to release a title, mine was out within about nine months (still a long time). I didn't like the cover design they produced, but my complaints were ignored, and I was left with a cover I didn't care for. I figured if that was the worst of it, it wasn't that big of a deal.

Within weeks of the release of the book, my editor left the publishing house. I never heard from a replacement editor or anyone there ever again. Nobody checked in to ask how things were going. No publicity support was offered. I was basically left on my own wondering if anyone at the publishing house even knew my name.

I did the promotion work as I continued to evolve my platform and the book hovered in Amazon's top-ten business marketing books for two solid years. Still, nobody from the publisher's offices ever reached out to me. Instead, I quietly received my royalty checks twice per year.

Shortly after that book release, I contacted an agent I'd met back at that writer's conference I had attended in 2005. I shared with her that I had built a platform and had sold a book on my own. She signed me right away, and we sold two more books over the next two years to different publishers.

DECIDING TRADITIONAL PUBLISHING NO LONGER WORKED FOR ME

During the production phase for the last book I sold to a traditional publisher, I received a call from the editor asking me to remove a chapter from the book. "We don't care which one, but we need to reduce page count to cut costs." I was mortified. How do you choose a chapter when they're all important? Didn't the publisher realize that cutting 20 pages from the book would only save pennies?

I had no choice but to comply, and ultimately turned lemons into lemonade. The end of the book featured a hearty resources section. I cut that section and turned it into a free download that readers could access upon registering on my website. (Today this is a strategy

I use in all of my books—offer one or more free downloads as a way to give readers extra value while also building my mailing list.)

But, removing that chapter left me with an awful feeling. I didn't like being reminded that ultimately the publisher had all the control. Worse, I was doing all the marketing and publicity work, yet they were reaping the majority of the rewards.

It was also frustrating to purchase copies of my own books for resale. I knew it only cost the publisher a few dollars each to print the books, yet I was forced to purchase them at a wholesale "discount" of 50% off the cover price—$10 each! I still find it outrageous that the publishers profit from the author's own purchases.

In fact, some publishers now put into their contracts that authors must commit to purchasing a certain number of copies. One author told me that he received a paltry book advance of $5,000 and was then required to purchase 1,000 copies of his own book upon its release—at a "wholesale" price of $9 each. When you do the math, you can see that he actually *lost money* on this so-called book deal. This once reputable publisher has now flipped its revenue model to actually generate income from the authors it grants these "book deals" to.

Eventually, I began questioning whether traditional publishing made sense for me. There was no arguing the math. I earned an average of $1 per book, while my self-published book was earning between $5 and $15 per copy, depending on whether it was sold through retailers or directly at speaking engagements. And while the novelty of seeing my books on store shelves was fun at first, that quickly wore off.

After much debate, I decided to fire my agent in the nicest way possible (we remain friends today), and I took back control of my own publishing destiny. I've since released five additional titles, for a grand total of nine books prior to this one, and I have never for a moment regretted my decision to self-publish.

Now I maintain all of the control (a win for this type-A personality), earn more royalties on sales, and earn 100% of my ebook sales. I would only receive a fraction of those revenues if I was with a traditional publishing house. I make the investment up front to ensure the highest-quality production, which includes solid editing and cover designs that I love. I was already doing all the marketing work. Now I no longer have to share the rewards of those efforts.

DOES TRADITIONAL PUBLISHING MAKE SENSE FOR YOU?

While many authors have a goal of getting traditionally published, we encourage you to think long and hard about whether or not it really makes sense for you. It's a myth that publishers will handle the marketing—this is incredibly rare. And if you're doing the work to build your platform and handle all of your marketing yourself anyway, you can potentially earn a lot more on your own. You can also work with a book distributor to get store placement if that's important to you, and you can negotiate deals to sell your books in bulk at a much higher profit than you ever could with traditional publishing.

Many authors have chosen the self-publishing route for all the same reasons and more. Bill Teie, who writes firefighting manuals and has contributed an interview to this book, turned down multiple six-figure book advance offers over the years because he couldn't make the math work. No matter how generous those book advances seemed, the publishers simply could not compete with the income he generated as a self-publisher. (Read his interview at the end of Chapter 9.)

If traditional publishing has been a goal for you, we encourage you to weigh the pros and cons. Speak with other authors who've gone down that path and find out what their experiences have been like. I suspect you'll hear many similar stories and perhaps you will realize that the benefits of self-publishing can be substantially greater when compared to what looms on the other side.

THE DOWNSIDE OF TRADITIONAL PUBLISHING— KEY POINTS TO REMEMBER

- It can take months or years to find an agent and/or publisher and then negotiate a deal.

- Low per-book royalties, averaging around $1 per copy.

- Book advances have decreased as traditional publishers have tried to figure out how to remain profitable in a competitive climate where self-publishers are gaining momentum.

- Some publishers may require you to commit to purchasing a large quantity of your own books at a "wholesale" rate—a rate that is actually profitable for the publisher and unfair to the author.

- The author loses all creative control. You may end up with a cover you don't like or editing that doesn't align with your vision. Large portions of your work can be modified, changed or deleted.

- It will likely take a year or more for your book to make it through production at a big publishing house and get released.

- Marketing support will probably be minimal, if any is offered at all.

- If your book makes it to bookstore shelves and doesn't sell within a couple of months, those books will get returned and the publisher will write you off faster than you can blink. When this happens, you can forget about future book deals with the publisher.

- You will still do most of the work yet receive few of the financial rewards.

Though our focus for this book is self-publishing, the final chapter covers how to land a traditional book deal. We understand that the goals are different for every author and we want you to be as successful as possible, no matter which publishing route you choose. See Chapter 19 if you want to learn more about how to get a traditional book deal.

CHAPTER 3
PROFIT OPPORTUNITIES WITH YOUR BOOK

As an author, you become an instant AUTHORity in your subject matter. We automatically give credibility to someone who has authored a book. We see them as successful and smart. They disproportionately represent the people in the front of the room at conferences.

So, with that bias built in, it is natural that people would believe that they would be successful if they can just publish a book. And while we are big believers in leveraging your book so you can move on to bigger things, you need to know that there is no magic in being a published author. You still have to do the work.

And here's another (unwelcome) dose of reality: unless you work your butt off, you won't sell many books. Every once in a while, you will stumble on someone who wrote a book that has become a standard in the industry or is required by a government agency. But the rest of us have to work for every sale.

Pay attention the next time a former United States president writes a book and hits the speaking trail. As long as he's running around from city to city making speeches, the book sells well. As soon as the speaking tour is over, those books are marked down and moved to the closeout table.

Now consider yourself. If an ex-president of the United States can't sell books without running all over the place speaking to groups, how can you expect to fare any better?

If you've done the hard work of building a following with a mailing list and a blog (or other audience engagement tools), then you have the right to go make speeches and hope that someone recommends your book. But chances are that you probably won't sell thousands, and maybe not even hundreds, unless you put continuous effort into marketing.

In an article published in *The Guardian,* a survey of more than 1,000 self-published authors revealed that the average earnings for those authors were just $500 per year. *Publishers Weekly* reported that for traditionally published books, the average number of copies sold over the lifetime of the book is just 3,000 copies. And for self-published authors, that number drops to a measly 250 copies over the lifetime of the book. The harsh reality is that books won't sell if you're not out building demand.

Karl's first book sold about 1,000 copies the first year at a profit of roughly $65 each. That's $65,000 and well beyond the industry standard. But it also took thousands of dollars in promotion and a four-country speaking tour to make that happen.

Here's the math: $90 retail price (specialty book) x 1,000 copies sold = $90,000. But Karl spent $25,000 to sell those 1,000 books, equaling an overhead of $25 per book—which is less than most books retail for.

Stephanie's first book also sold about 1,000 copies the first year in print and digital formats (PDF back then) at an average profit of about $11, which netted a grand total of $11,000 in profit. Her primary focus was online sales and reaching her target audience with content—and keep in mind that this was before social media came along. But she had an audience of potential buyers because she did the work to build her platform—and so can you!

GOOD NEWS FOR AUTHORS

Karl's most successful book has grossed about $400,000 in sales over five years. Every other book has grossed at least $50,000 within the first three years of publication. Most of them have been over the $100,000 mark.

Karl's sales figures demonstrate the power of a niche as well as the benefits of finding an audience willing to pay more than the average. Stephanie's books are priced much lower than Karl's so her book revenues are less than his and more typical for standard trade nonfiction.

The good news is that you can earn money with your books, but there are some steps you'll need to take to do so.

Karl makes a living by writing a minimum of one book per year. He works his tail off writing, blogging, speaking, training, doing webinars, promoting podcasts, mailing out postcards, begging, pleading, and selling from the front of the room. In addition, books are not his only revenue stream; the book is one of more than a dozen ways Karl earns his living.

In 2011, Karl set a goal to spend ten years writing one book a year and making an average of $100,000 gross sales per book. At that point, he'll see how much residual income he can make from his list of titles. (So far, he has averaged almost two books per year, and seven of them have reached that income target.) But he also takes a *huge* percentage of that money and pumps it into marketing his books and his business.

Until 2013, Stephanie was also releasing one book each year. Then life took a turn when her husband died unexpectedly and she realized that having multiple revenue streams, along with an administrative support team to help keep the business running, were essential. The point is that you can set goals—and you should—but life may throw you some curveballs along the way.

Writing multiple books can be part of a great long-term strategy to grow your audience, sell your past audience new books, and uncover new marketing opportunities, but it's not the only way to go. If you want to publish just one book and sell the heck out of it, you can do that too. There are plenty of people who have built careers around a single book they wrote. Either way, we recommend building additional revenue streams into your author-business model.

MINING FOR REVENUE OPPORTUNITIES

Think of your book as an entry point into your author-business. When we read a good book, we often become bonded to the author. We feel a personal connection, as if we know the author (or would like to). A book is a tool for building alliances, creating fans, and increasing revenues.

So, when a reader finds value inside your book's pages, she will naturally be interested in visiting your website, blog, social media, and other resources that you have available (including products and services). The book is just the first step in a long road that you can create for your readers to journey through.

Following are some of the benefits of authorship and ways you might want to expand and build a profitable author-business.

DEVELOP PROGRAMS THAT SUPPORT YOUR BOOK

If you don't already have programs that support the theories in your book, perhaps you should. Whether you ask them to or not, readers will call, write, and send emails inquiring about how to implement the strategies in your book. Consider developing coaching programs, training packages, consulting services, and other services that complement your subject matter.

SHARPEN YOUR COMPETITIVE EDGE

We all face competition, and if you want to crush yours, a book can get the job done quickly. Think about it from the consumer point of view. Let's say that you want to hire a personal trainer. You interview a trainer with the typical credentials. He's friendly, says the right things, and his pricing is about average.

Then you interview a second trainer. He is also friendly and says the right things. At the end of your meeting, he hands you a copy of his book, *The Healthy, Wealthy, and Happy Life Program*. It has an appealing cover design, and he even autographs it for you while you watch.

Who are you most likely going to hire?

There is nothing like a book to impress prospects and close deals. Give away books like you hand out business cards and your business is sure to grow. Often, simply adding the cover of your book to your business card can be effective.

EARN HIGHER FEES

If you are a service provider, such as a consultant, coach, graphic artist, doctor, therapist, financial advisor, or other business professional, your book gives you a license to charge higher rates. It all comes back to that credibility factor. You are not just an average expert in your field, you are a *published authority*. Of course your rates are higher than your competitors'.

The idea of raising rates makes some people uncomfortable. The reality is that as an author, most people are going to expect your rates to be higher than the rest. If you've written a book and yet you remain the low-price leader in your industry, it doesn't quite add up. You are an authority in your field! If you wanted to hire Tony Robbins to coach you on success, would you expect to pay him $50 per hour? Heck no! You would pay a premium rate because he's an expert who must be in high demand.

Another challenge in raising prices is the fear that you will lose business. And the truth is that you may lose some clients (though if you're truly demonstrating value, this becomes less of an issue). But keep in mind that with higher rates it takes fewer clients to earn the same income. And sometimes raising your rates can also improve the quality of the clients you attract because there is a perception of value. If something costs more, it must be better, right?

The bottom line is that your income should increase as your author status drives up demand for your services.

CAPTURE HARD-TO-GET APPOINTMENTS

Want to speak with the CEO, head of Human Resources, a political leader, or some other hard-to-reach contact? Send a copy of your book along with a personal note. Odds are much better that your next call will go through. "This is Annie Author calling . . ."

We've all heard of gimmicks in the sales world. One of my favorite examples that I heard several years ago was when a salesperson sent his prospect a VCR with a video inside (the VCR is a good indicator of how old this trick is). He stuck a note on top that said, "Play me." The package was bulky, which made it far more likely to get opened than a sales letter shoved in an envelope. Even the most guarded administrative assistant with strict gatekeeping orders is bound to inform her boss that a VCR arrived in the mail.

Though it was a creative idea that actually worked for that particular salesperson, it was also an expensive gamble to send a package like that. (And today if you sent a large electronic device to a prospect, the recipient's mailroom might call in the bomb squad, so we don't recommend going this route.)

With a book, your hard costs are the book itself, which you should be able to purchase at wholesale for just a few dollars, and postage. So, even if it costs a grand total of $10 to send a package, ask yourself how much this kind of marketing is worth to you. If you reel in the business of a prestigious client that you wouldn't otherwise have had, the return on investment is HUGE.

When sending out copies to cold prospects (people you don't know), it is wise to follow up with the recipient. Send a short email asking if he/she received your package. We have both personally received a lot of unsolicited books, primarily from authors seeking endorsements of some kind. The ones that get our attention have several qualities in common:

- The book arrives with a personal note from the author. The author gets bonus points if the note indicates that he/she has read or benefited from my books, blog, website, etc. That instantly creates a bond between us and inspires me to want to help.

- The book is somehow related to my industry. Children's books and pizza cookbooks are nice, but they have nothing to do with either of our businesses or expertise. It would make no sense for us to endorse them. However, if an author wants to pitch us on her personal chef services and sends along her cookbook, now she's got our attention!

- The book is professionally produced. Every self-published book should look like it came from a big New York publishing house. It should be professionally edited with an impressive cover design and quality binding.

    Someone once sent me a "book" bound like a booklet from Kinkos. I love booklets; they can be great promotional tools. But I'm sorry to say that you can't call it a book. Aside from that, the production quality was beyond poor. Images were hand-drawn by someone who clearly wasn't an artist. She would have been better served to use some basic clip art—and called it what it was: a booklet!

- The author sends a follow-up email within a couple of weeks of the package arriving. Again, here the author is attempting to make a personal connection with me (not sending some form letter that is clearly going out to tons of people). Receiving a brief, friendly email is a gentle nudge that inspires a desire to respond.

GENERATE REFERRALS

Word of mouth is arguably one of the best kinds of marketing on the planet. When someone recommends a product, restaurant, book, or service, we buy. Whether that recommendation comes from a friend, a business associate, a magazine article, or a television show, consumers are influenced by the opinions of others.

A good book is going to naturally generate recommendations from readers. Think about the last book that you read and loved. How many people did you tell about it? If your book is doing its job and leading people back to your website, it can create a referral pipeline for your business.

Another way to generate referrals with your book is to introduce it to people who are influential in your industry. Several years ago, a family law attorney sent copies of her parenting book to marriage therapists all over town. Since therapists were often talking to her potential clients—people headed for divorce—she took a chance that the book might make an impression. Her law practice quickly became the largest of its kind in her city.

A side note here is that her book had nothing to do with the legal system or her law practice. It was a parenting guide—a topic that was *indirectly* related to her business. Regardless, she found a way to generate referrals by sharing her book with influential people who could send referral business her way.

For some businesses, it takes just a few good referral sources to grow a company quickly. A book gives you the opportunity to multiply those referral sources in a big way.

STAND OUT AT TRADE SHOWS

If you host a booth at trade shows, your booth won't be ordinary once you showcase your book and your work as an author. Prospects and potential alliance partners will be eager to meet the author.

To increase exposure, have a sign that reads "Author Book Signing" and offer to autograph any books that you sell (or give away). Even if book sales aren't your primary goal, it is highly likely that you will capture attention. Attendees will ask questions about your book and also about your business. You can also use copies of your book as prizes for a drawing that you host.

By the way, corporations may also want to buy your book as a giveaway for their own trade show events. Mugs, pens, and squishy balls are boring trade show swag. But if you've authored a book on healthy living, a vitamin supplement company or an athletic shoe maker might love to buy hundreds or even thousands of copies and give your book away at events. (Hint: Upsell them on the opportunity to place their logo on your cover. It's incredibly easy to produce a special edition print run of a self-published book.)

GENERATE PASSIVE INCOME FROM INFORMATION PRODUCTS

As you build a following of loyal readers, selling information products can become a lucrative passive income stream. Information products include ebooks, special reports, workbooks, audio recordings, whitepapers, teleseminar recordings, spreadsheets, templates, and virtually any way that you can compile and deliver information. Information products are often quicker and easier to produce than a book, and they can perfectly complement your efforts as an author.

Perhaps one of the greatest advantages of information products is that once they are created and the distribution process is automated, they can sell around the clock with minimal effort, provided you are driving traffic to your online store.

Giveaways are another fantastic use for info products. For example, you can reward new subscribers to your email list by giving away an ebook, a few sample chapters from your book, or a short video tutorial. Or you could send your ebook to other business owners and allow them to distribute it for free to their audience, provided all of your contact information is included. This strategy will ultimately bring you new customers and that all-important exposure to your audience.

 PRO TIPS: *Develop information product ideas.*

- ✓ Conduct a survey with your readers and ask them what information they need or would like to know. Use the results to form new product ideas.

- ✓ Make a list of the most common questions your readers and target audience have asked you, and then consider what kinds of products you could create to address those questions.

✓ Teach people how to do what you do.

✓ Create a directory or database. Do you have a list of 50 or more resources that people in your industry need? Sell that list!

✓ Develop a companion workbook that complements your book.

✓ Offer training via a teleseminar or webinar series.

✓ Develop checklists, templates, worksheets, and other handy tools your audience can use.

✓ Produce a video of a demonstration, speech, or technique.

BUILD A CERTIFICATION PROGRAM

You can use your book as the foundation to develop your own certification program and recruit agents who deliver services under your brand, while they also promote your book and generate revenue for your business.

Jim Horan is a small-business consultant who wrote a book about a proprietary process he used with his clients. He self-published *The One Page Business Plan for the Creative Entrepreneur,* and soon fellow consultants were asking him if they could teach his processes to their own clients. In response, Jim built a consultant certification program through his website: OnePageBusinessPlan.com. Consultants pay around $3,500 for a week-long webinar-based training program, and once they pass the certification exam, they go out in the world and teach Jim's processes—while promoting his brand and selling his books. He's certified hundreds of *One Page Business Plan* consultants to date.

Simply brilliant, don't you think? You can read an interview with Jim at the end of this chapter.

SCHEDULE SPEAKING ENGAGEMENTS

If you want to grow your author-business and reach a lot of people quickly, consider developing your skills as a professional speaker. There are dozens of trade organizations in every major city that need speakers for their weekly or monthly meetings, as well as their annual conferences. You can leverage the instant credibility that comes with being an author and use your book as a door-opener for speaking opportunities.

Start by offering to speak for free to gain experience (and sell books at the back of the room), and then work your way up to earning a fee. Professional speakers can earn fees ranging from $1,500 to $10,000 and up. Even if you never charge a speaking fee, when done right, these engagements can generate plenty of revenue opportunities from back-of-the-room sales.

You might be surprised by how quickly your business can grow as a result of your speaking engagements and that you can sell thousands of books along the way. Soon, you may find that you don't have to go looking for speaking opportunities. As you build a reputation and your platform, speaking invitations will come to you.

BECOME AN INSTRUCTOR

Authors are welcomed as instructors at adult learning programs, community centers, and many colleges. These organizations will promote your classes through their catalogs and direct mail campaigns, and that publicity can bring great exposure and new business opportunities. Even if your class only has ten or twenty students, being seen in the program catalog by thousands of readers can impact your business and your book sales.

HOLD YOUR OWN EVENTS

Authors like Jack Canfield, Tony Robbins, Brené Brown, and countless others leverage their notoriety and experience to host their own revenue-generating events and workshops. Events can range from half-day meetings in a rented office space to week-long events at a hotel or even on a cruise ship. For some, holding annual events can be the biggest revenue-generator of the year, surpassing revenues from book sales and all other business activities.

SELL LARGE QUANTITIES

Identify the target audience for your book and look for opportunities to land bulk sales agreements. For example, a trade association could purchase and give away copies of your book to new members. A corporation could use your book as training material or as a giveaway at its annual conference. A nonprofit group might use your book as a promotional tool or even a revenue-generator by purchasing quantities from you at a discount and selling individual copies at full price. A bank might want to offer your book as a bonus for those opening new business accounts or applying for a home loan.

Consider the types of organizations that could benefit from your book. Offer deep discounts on bulk orders and create a win-win situation.

UNCOVER OPPORTUNITIES YOU DIDN'T EVEN KNOW ABOUT

Over the years, Karl and Stephanie have each launched a variety of services, including their own publishing companies, as a result of listening to their readers. We pay attention to what kinds of questions readers ask us and how we can solve their problems. The answers to their questions can become blog content, book content, new products, new services, and much more.

There is a good chance that writing a book is going to help you uncover revenue opportunities. That may mean that you develop new consulting programs, workshops, workbooks, ebooks, or even a series of future books. Welcome feedback from your readers because it reflects their needs and gives you an opportunity to address them.

THE SECRET TO A PROFITABLE AUTHOR-BUSINESS

Success with book sales is relative. You may consider yourself a success if you sell 1,000 copies in five years. And if you do, you'll be ahead of the self-publishing sales curve. Or perhaps your goal is to sell 3,000 or 10,000 or even 100,000 books. Good for you! Aim high and then do the work needed to get there.

The same is true when you're building a business around your book. You'll need to do the work, but your efforts can absolutely pay off if you're committed to doing what it takes to be successful.

BUILD A REVENUE PLAN FOR YOUR BOOK:
Questions to Ask Yourself

- How much will my book sell for?

- What are other books in my space selling for?

- Who is my ideal buyer?

- How will I market the book? Online, through speaking, direct mail campaigns, catalogs, trade associations, etc.?

- What formats will I offer my book in? Paperback, hardcover, Kindle, e-reader, PDF, audio?

- Can I reach my audience in other countries?

- Should my book be translated into any other languages?

- What annual sales goal do I want to set for my book?

- How much can I *realistically* earn from the book each year?

- Will my book be part of a series?

- Where can I sell copies my book? Retail stores, restaurants, pet supply, libraries, schools, corporations?

- Where could I sell my book in bulk?

- What companies would be interested in my book for their internal staff?

- What companies would be interested in my book for their own customers/clients?

BUILD A REVENUE PLAN FOR YOUR AUTHOR-BUSINESS:
Questions to Ask Yourself

- What problems can I solve for my audience with products and services that I create? In other words, what are their needs and challenges and how I can serve them?

- Do I want to offer consulting or coaching services?

- What would my services look like?

- How much should I charge?

- How much do my competitors charge?

- Do I want to become a speaker?

- Will I speak for free, charge a fee, or both?

- Realistically, how often would I want to travel for speaking opportunities?

- Who would likely hire me to speak? (Companies, trade associations, nonprofits, hospitals, schools, churches, etc.)

- What kinds of information products could I create for my audience? (Reports, white papers, databases, audio recordings, training videos, workbooks, templates, checklists, etc.)

- Should I offer online or in-person courses?

- What similar courses are currently available?

- What course topics are missing in the marketplace?

- What topics should my courses cover?

- Could I develop a process that would work as a certification program?

- Who would participate in my certification program and how would I reach them?

- What is missing in my industry that I can offer?

PRO TIP: *Be a problem solver.*

To serve your audience and get them to invest in your book and related products and services, you need to deliver value. Start by identifying the needs and challenges of the people in your audience. What questions do they ask frequently? What concerns do they have? Once you understand their pain points, you can then provide solutions to their challenges through your books, products, training programs, and services.

"Are you paralyzed with fear? That's a good sign. Fear is good. Like self-doubt, fear is an indicator. Fear tells us what we have to do. Remember one rule of thumb: the more scared we are of a work or calling, the more sure we can be that we have to do it."

—Steven Pressfield

AUTHOR INTERVIEW

Name: Jim Horan

Book Titles:
The One Page Business Plan for the Creative Entrepreneur
The One Page Business Plan for the Busy Executive
The One Page Business Plan for Nonprofit Executives
The One Page Business Plan for the Professional Consultant
The One Page Business Plan, Financial Services Edition
The One Page Business Plan for Women in Business

Website: OnePageBusinessPlan.com

Can you tell us about your publishing journey and why you chose to self-publish your books?

I never had intentions of being an author. I was kicked out of corporate America where I had been a corporate accountant, controller, and CFO. It was in 1990, on April Fool's Day of all days, and the separation from corporate was difficult and traumatic for me. After that I was looking for a job, and then one day a colleague who owned his own consulting business called and said, "Jim, I've got a client that really needs help with planning and budgeting. Would you be willing to give him a call and see if you could help?"

I did, and I found myself becoming an accidental entrepreneur, and an accidental consultant. I got my first client, then the second, and a third, and the next thing I knew I had a consulting business called Rent-a-CFO. It was a rather blasphemous title twenty-five years ago. Today there are all sorts of fractional CFOs and marketing directors. The One Page Business Plan was conceived in the early days of my Rent-a-CFO practice

After I mocked up the first version of The One Page Business Plan, I took it to my entrepreneur support group and said, "I'd like your feedback on this wild idea." They replied, "Jim, you've got something, and you need to do something with this."

When I asked what they meant, they said I should take up public speaking, but I told them public speaking terrified me. Then a good friend told me to just get over it. He introduced me to the last five places he had spoken at and my speaking career was launched.

As soon as I began speaking, audiences asked me if I had a book. My market was speaking to me and telling me what they wanted. I thought about it and went back to my business group to ask what I should do. They of course told me that I needed to write a book. I said, "Look, you don't understand, I got Cs and Ds in English. I'm the last guy on Earth that should be writing a book."

They introduced me to the Bay Area Independent Publishers Association where I learned about self-publishing. I also hired a writing coach and then I was off to the races to write a book. Although it was a very slow process, I started and stopped half a dozen times. It took me over three years to finally get my book finished.

What kind of business are you in now and how has your book helped to grow your business?

The book completely transformed my business. I moved from being a solo consultant and independent CFO to launching The One Page Business Plan company. To date I've published six different versions of the book.

When my first book, *The One Page Business Plan for The Creative Entrepreneur,* got into the hands of corporate America they started knocking on my door and saying they wanted One Page Business Plans, and they also wanted software. Given what had happened with my public speaking and audiences asking for a book, I knew I was in trouble.

All I could think was, *Oh no, the market wants software*. So, I went back to my support group and they said, "Jim, go create software!" I told them I didn't know how to do that and I didn't have that kind of money. Their response: "Jim, go explore it, go research it, you know lots of different people, don't dismiss this request from your market."

As it turned out, the answer was right in front of me. One of my clients was one of the early web software developers. I went to them and I said, "Hey, I'd like to brainstorm something with you." By the way, I think it's really important for us as nonfiction authors to reach out into our community, to our tribe, and say, "I've got an idea and I'd like your feedback."

Within 30 minutes of approaching my client, we had brainstormed the basic framework and concepts for a cloud-based The One Page Planning and Performance Management System. They designed and built it, and at an affordable price. We put the system into the marketplace in January of 2000.

During the final design and prototyping phase, I went to some of my friends and colleagues at the Institute of Management Consultants and said, "I'm building a web-based system for The One Page Business Plan. Would you give me your feedback?" They agreed, and then something amazing happened. These consultants asked if they could have The One Page System in their consulting toolkit; they wanted to offer this system and their consulting services to their own clients. It was unbelievable. Of course, I said yes!

So, I designed an affiliate program for consultants, coaches, and business advisors with training, certification and licensing. Consultants paid $3,000 each to get trained in our methodology and systems, and the fee included a license to market and sell One Page Business Plan consulting engagements. Over the last 18 years we've recruited, trained, and licensed over 600 management consultants all around the world.

By the way, I've been involved in an entrepreneur support group (like a mastermind group) in one form or another for a long time, and as you can see, it absolutely transformed my business. My suggestion to all entrepreneurs and writers is that you should not try to go it alone.

Find a support group like the Nonfiction Authors Association. We need to have people in our tribe who are doing what we're doing so we can support each other.

What have been some book marketing strategies that have generated the best results for you?

Hands down, public speaking has been my best strategy. Every nonfiction author needs to be out speaking, and you don't have to be good at speaking! I still speak with "uhs" and "ahs," and I put my hands in my pockets and so forth. But when nonfiction authors have valuable information and get up in front of audiences to share that information freely—without selling—people in the audience will buy their books and will also buy their professional services.

Also, my favorite word in business is "association." What I have learned over the years is that the most successful people in business are actively involved, and have memberships in, one or more associations because they need a place where they can go and learn and share with each other. So, whatever area of expertise you have, there are one or more associations that are natural markets for you.

I encourage you to reach out to current clients, former clients, former employers, friends, people at the same church, etc. and ask, "I'm curious, what association are you personally involved with?" An even better second question is, "I'm curious, are you involved in the leadership of any associations?"

The goal is to have the people that know, like, and respect you to know what you are currently doing and what your expertise is so they will naturally come to the conclusion you can be of service to them and their association! When that happens, your friends and colleagues will begin to introduce you to influential people in their tribe who will want to get to know you! When that happens, do not be surprised when you get invited to speak locally, regionally, nationally, and internationally. Being in service of the people in our tribe is the single most powerful thing I've done to create visibility as a nonfiction author. I have learned speaking at association events is magical!

Something I never could have imagined happened as a result of my speaking at associations; associations began to build The One Page Business Plan into their management and executive development programs. This adds up to several thousand books each year purchased by these different associations.

Is there anything that you would do differently next time, or any hard lessons that you learned?

Well, I should have gotten more help with my first book, and should I write another one that is the first thing I will do. At the moment I don't have plans to write another book, but we know how that goes for authors, it just kind of happens. If I do I would hire a coach and would consider working with a ghostwriter to speed up the process. Three and a half years to write my first book was way too long.

One thing that I feel good about is that I actually did something with my book. I learned through my local publishers' association that only one percent of books published ever sell 3,000 copies, and that's because authors kill themselves getting their book written and then think the job is done and they stop there.

What I've learned is that you need to do *something* with your book, and then you need to do the next *something*, and then the next *something*. Does it help if you have a mailing list? You bet. Does it help if you have a plan? Absolutely. But the plan doesn't need to be perfect. After 21 years, I'm still doing the next *something* with my books, and I have no intention of stopping!

What advice would you offer to new authors?

Your book is a business; treat it like a business. Like I said, just go do *something* with your book. Public speaking is very important. I feel that every nonfiction author should be at the front of the room, not the back of the room.

I meet hundreds and hundreds of consultants and coaches and business advisors every year and too many of them act in a self-serving, self-focused manner. A better approach, and one of my favorite questions to ask people, is, "How can I be of service to you?"

When I asked this question, inevitably I found people will tell me where they need help and why. I frequently do some free/pro bono work, but selectively and strategically. Those that need more than a little help are very frequently ready to reach for their checkbook. But the key is this: you have expertise, you have knowledge, and the universe needs it. There are people out there who need your expertise. Go share it in as many different ways as you can. People will begin to talk about you behind your back . . . and you are going to love it!

CHAPTER 4
CHOOSE A NICHE AUDIENCE

When you're setting out to launch your book into the world, you will be faced with a lot of competition. There are millions of book titles available today, which means that book categories are jam-packed with options for readers.

At this very moment, here are the total number of titles listed on Amazon for various nonfiction book categories:

- Biography and Memoir: 507,000

- Business and Money: 1.8 million

- Computers and Technology: 415,000

- Health, Fitness and Dieting: 676,000

- Parenting and Relationship: 230,000

- Reference: 2.8 million

- Religion and Spirituality: 1.3 million

- Self-Help: 423,000

Of course, there are also sub-categories on Amazon, which help ever so slightly. But the competition is still incredibly steep there, too.

Here are some sub-categories listed under Biography and Memoir:

- Arts and Literature: 103,000

- Historical: 77,000

- Leaders and Notable People: 112,000

- Memoirs (General): 133,000

- Travelers and Explorers: 32,000

- True Crime: 37,000

Amazon even has some sub-sub categories, which are *slightly* less competitive.

Under Business and Money, here are some sub-sub categories:

- Business and Money > Marketing and Sales > Advertising: 20,000

- Business and Money > Marketing and Sales > Biographies: 13,000

- Business and Money > Marketing and Sales > Sales and Selling: 16,000

- Business and Money > Small Business and Entrepreneurship > Home-Based: 11,000

- Business and Money > Small Business and Entrepreneurship > Marketing: 3,000

As you can see, even the smallest sub-categories carry tremendous competition.

What does this mean for you? It means it is imperative you find a way to make your book stand out against the rest. And the best way to do that is to identify a niche topic and get clear about your audience.

WHY NICHES RULE

Let's say you're authoring a memoir. Considering there are 133,000 memoirs on Amazon right now, there is little chance your title will rise to the top unless you are a celebrity, a controversial politician or you do something regrettable on a reality TV show. Your next best option? Develop a clear niche focus.

Glennon Doyle's *Love Warrior* is a memoir of her husband's affair and the resulting efforts to repair her marriage. According to StatisticBrain.com, an astonishing 41% of marriages will experience infidelity. That creates a lot of potential readers and is one of many reasons why Doyle's book became a hot bestseller (it was also well-written, the author has built a solid platform, and then Oprah shouted praise from the Twitter rooftops).

Also, note that though the core target may be women impacted by infidelity, it did not prevent other women from reading the book. In fact, the fear of infidelity and its aftermath may have also compelled such a substantial reading audience.

Oftentimes the book title and positioning can capture a niche audience perfectly. Between 2002 and 2007, Rick Warren's *The Purpose-Driven Life* sold over 30 million copies. Why? Because it appealed to people who were seeking some spiritual direction. Imagine how differently this book might have fared had Warren titled it something like *Basic Christianity Principles*. Did that make you want to yawn? Instead, the title—and ultimately the niche focus—addressed a specific need Warren saw in readers.

The Four-Hour Workweek: Escape the 9 to 5, Live Anywhere and Join the New Rich by Tim Ferriss is another example of a title that attracted its target audience in droves. Disgruntled corporate employees were the niche focus for this one. One Gallup survey indicated that as many as 70% of people are disengaged from their jobs. Since its release in 2009, *The Four-Hour Workweek* has sold over a million copies and been translated into 35 languages.

By the way, Ferriss reportedly considered several initial book titles and purchased Google ads to test and see which title drove the most traffic. Titles in the running included *Broadband and White Sand* and *Millionaire Chameleon*. While his target audience remained the same, clearly, he chose a much more powerful title thanks to testing to see how many clicks each title generated with Google ads. Note that his title offered some big promises, enticing readers who might have otherwise passed over yet another book on how to start a business.

THE POWER OF A NICHE

Karl's audience is Information Technology (IT) consultants—people who own technology companies. He teaches them how to grow their businesses. It's a small community, which allows Karl—and his books and related products and services—to stand out.

He began by establishing himself as an AUTHORity in his community. Having owned his own IT company for many years allowed Karl to relate to his target audience and lead by example. In addition to books, Karl sells over 100 digital products from his website, he hosts live events around the globe, offers online courses, and he works with corporate sponsors who want to reach his audience. His books are an essential piece of the puzzle, but they're only the beginning.

Stephanie built her early author career around helping entrepreneurs start and grow their businesses. Over time she discovered that many in her audience had questions about writing and publishing books. Because she has always had a heart for working with writers and people who want to make a difference in the world, she eventually shifted her focus away from the small business audience (a rather broad category with lots of competition) and chose to work exclusively with nonfiction authors (a significant niche with surprisingly little competition).

Many of her previous tribe followed her over to the nonfiction world because there was some natural crossover between the two topics. Narrowing her focus to a niche topic—one she was passionate about—made it easy for her to stand out as a leader in the nonfiction publishing community.

Niches rule! They allow us to rise to the top of the crowded book marketplace. They help readers better relate to us. They help us sell books.

Karl could have decided to become a general business consultant. He certainly had the experience of running businesses and could offer his expertise to all kinds of companies. But he chose to focus on the small niche of IT consultants—and that decision has paid off many times over.

Stephanie could have decided to focus on publishing in general, as most of her peers have done. But her passion was with nonfiction authors and she saw a need in the marketplace. As she was speaking at writers' conferences and events, she noticed that nonfiction was rarely addressed. She suspected that nonfiction authors were feeling left out, and her hunch was right. It's one of the reasons the Nonfiction Authors Association community has grown at lightning speed. There was almost no competition because nearly every other writers' group gives most of its attention to the fiction writers.

How can you narrow your focus and carve out a niche for yourself?

EXAMPLES OF AUTHORS WITH NICHE AUDIENCES

Shasta Nelson was a life coach who noticed that many of her female clients yearned to have more friends but didn't know how to go about developing new friendships since it tends to get harder as we get older. In response, she launched a website called GirlfriendCircles.com, which essentially worked like an online dating site for women's friendships. Because of her platform, Shasta landed traditional book deals for her books: *Friendships Don't Just Happen: The Guide to Creating a Meaningful Circle of Girlfriends* and *Frientimacy: How to Deepen Friendships for Lifelong Health and Happiness.*

Today, Shasta is known as "America's Friendship Expert." She's been featured on *The Today Show, Good Morning America, Katie*

Couric, and more. She is also a paid speaker and consultant on the topic of friendship.

Dana Manciagli is a former corporate executive who decided to leave her lucrative career behind and become a job-search coach. She self-published her book *Cut the Crap, Get a Job,* and landed a column writing about job-search advice for *The Business Journals* newspaper franchise. She also developed an online self-study course for job seekers, which sells for just under $1,000. In the first six months of the course launch, she sold over 50 seats.

She followed that success by reaching out to a large technology company and asking if they would sponsor seats in her course for military personnel coming out of service and seeking civilian jobs. They agreed to purchase her course, at a discounted rate of $600 per seat, and she inked a high six-figure agreement that put her business on track to become a seven-figure empire. It all started with her self-published book.

Rob Ludlow runs a website called BackyardChickens.com, a hub where visitors discuss the joys and trials of raising chickens at home. Would you believe this niche site attracts over *one million* unique visitors per month?

The site doesn't sell chicken feed or chicken coops or anything at all, beyond an annual calendar and some fun branded merchandise. Because of the incredible level of traffic generated, Rob earns a substantial living from ads placed throughout the site (while working a part-time schedule and enjoying the rewards of his efforts).

Rob is co-author of *Raising Chickens for Dummies* and *Gardening with Free-Range Chickens for Dummies*, and he attracted both of the book opportunities because of his website and the fact that he is THE leader in the backyard chickens niche.

Oftentimes the smallest niches yield the biggest rewards.

HOW TO FIND YOUR NICHE

Hopefully by now you're starting to see why claiming a niche is so important. Without one, your book risks becoming just another title in a sea of options.

Let's say you're writing a memoir, which has a strong focus on your journey living with diabetes. Guess who could make up your target audience? Other people living with diabetes. According to Diabetes.org, that adds up to over 29 million Americans. So, you could promote yet another general memoir, or you could focus your efforts on connecting with the diabetes community.

The same rules apply for other genres. If you're writing a self-help guide about how to live a happier life, you need to find a way to stand out. Could your target audience be single moms? (According to SingleMotherGuide.com there are more than 9 million single moms in the U.S.) Could your audience be those suffering from depression (a whopping 350 million people)? Or could you focus on people who work in a specific industry, such as dentists or lawyers or restaurant workers?

Ideally your niche audience is something you should determine before your book is even written—because then you'll know exactly whom you're writing it for. Once you have a clearly defined niche, everything you do—from the blog posts you write to the content you speak about and share via social media—should appeal to your audience.

By the way, Stephanie wrote a book on this topic a few years back: *Own Your Niche: Hype-Free Internet Marketing Tactics to Establish Authority in Your Field and Promote Your Service-Based Business.*

In case it's not yet clear, we firmly believe there are two keys to a profitable author-business:

1. An engaged niche audience

2. Lots of hustle

When you combine these two elements, you have the potential to make your wildest dreams a reality.

CLAIM YOUR NICHE: *Questions to Ask Yourself*

- Who can relate to my story and the information I have to share?

- Who else has been through similar experiences?

- How can I help or inspire others?

- Who do I *want* to inspire, help, or entertain?

- What audience can I find from my personal background? (Were you previously enlisted in the military or serve as a kids' sports coach? Did you work in high tech or health care? Are you a schoolteacher, dog walker, or a federal employee? All of these can be niches all their own.)

- Are there clients I've worked with in the past that could become a niche of their own?

- Are there people/clients I *don't* want to target or work with?

- What causes do I care about? (Are you involved in a nonprofit that supports mental health awareness, animal rescue, domestic violence, or children's issues?)

- Where do I want my books to be sold? (For example, if you're aiming at colleges, your audience might be young hotel-industry professionals or people starting out in the finance industry.)

- What readers would I most enjoy working with?

- Where do I want to speak?

- How do I want to make a difference in the world?

- What competition exists in my space?

- What is missing in my space?

- How could I bridge a gap or bring something new to my audience?

- How could I narrow my focus even more? (Remember, Karl could have become a consultant to all businesses, but he chose to focus on IT business owners. Stephanie could have become an educator for all writers, but she chose to focus on nonfiction. Often, the narrower your focus, the easier it will be to stand out.)

"The more you learn, the more you earn."
—Warren Buffett

CHAPTER 5
WRITE YOUR NONFICTION MANUSCRIPT

Before you start writing your next manuscript, it's important to determine how your book will be different from others in your genre. You can search online (Amazon is a great source) for other books covering similar topics to see what's already been done. Then you can determine how your book will offer something new or fill in a gap that's missing.

When we set out to write this book, we clearly knew that there were already many books available on book publishing. But our research showed that none of them specifically addressed the unique benefits and profit opportunities for *nonfiction*. Knowing this made our job much easier. It gave us assurance that there was a need in the marketplace for this book and also helped give us direction for shaping the manuscript.

Just as you would use a map to find your way to a destination, you need to plan your route when writing your book.

Ask yourself these questions:

- What topics are missing in my genre?

- What do my readers care about?

- How is my perspective or process different from the rest?

- How can I offer help in a way my fellow authors haven't yet?

- What struggles can I help my readers solve?

- How can I help improve readers' lives in some way?

- How am I different now than I was at the beginning of my book?

- What lessons have I learned and how can they help others? (For memoir writers.)

CHOOSE YOUR PROCESS

You don't have to be a professionally trained writer to develop a book. If writing doesn't come naturally for you, here are several options:

- Hire a ghostwriter (visit associationofghostwriters.org).

- Enlist one or more co-authors.

- Dictate your book with audio translation software such as Dragon Naturally Speaking, or record yourself and have the recordings transcribed.

- Get your thoughts on paper and hire a professional editor to turn it into a manuscript.

- Work with a book coach to guide you through the process.

- Assemble an anthology of contributions from others.

SELECT A WORKING TITLE

Choosing a title can be tough for any author, new or experienced. A title will almost always change several times before going to press, which is why those of us in publishing call it a "working title." Do your best to make your title something that will quickly describe the scope of your book in a catchy or immediately clear way, like *Eating My Way Through Rome* or *7 Ways to Organize and De-Clutter Your Home*.

Subtitles are extremely important in nonfiction because they further provide the reader with a better understanding of the book. Also, your subtitle is a great place to incorporate keywords that your potential readers would use to find your book. For example, if you're writing a book about retirement planning for single parents, your title might look something like this:

Retire Solo: The Single Parent's Guide to Retirement Planning, Saving, and Living Happily Ever After on Your Own

A title for any kind of how-to book should also include a *promise* to the reader. What benefits will readers gain from the book? How will it change or improve readers' lives in some way? Examples:

- *The 7 Habits of Highly Effective People: Powerful Lessons in Personal Change* by Stephen Covey

- *The 5 Love Languages: The Secret to Love That Lasts* by Gary Chapman

- *You Are a Badass: How to Stop Doubting Your Greatness and Start Living an Awesome Life* by Jen Sincero

- *A Whole New Mind: Why Right-Brainers Will Rule the Future* by Daniel Pink

- *The Happiness Advantage: How a Positive Brain Fuels Success in Work and Life* by Shawn Achor

- *Goddesses Never Age: The Secret Prescription for Radiance, Vitality, and Well-Being* by Dr. Christiane Northrup

- *Delivering Happiness: A Path to Profits, Passion, and Purpose* by Tony Hsieh

- *Tears to Triumph: The Spiritual Journey from Suffering to Enlightenment* by Marianne Williamson

- *Anxious for Nothing: Finding Calm in a Chaotic World* by Max Lucado
- *Dying to Be Me: My Journey from Cancer to Near Death to True Healing* by Anita Moorjani
- *Eat Dirt: Why Leaky Gut May Be the Root Cause of Your Health Problems and 5 Surprising Steps to Cure It* by Dr. Josh Axe
- *Dealing with People You Can't Stand: How to Bring Out the Best in People at Their Worst* by Rick Brinkman and Dr. Rick Kirschner
- *What Color Is Your Parachute? A Practical Manual for Job-Hunters and Career-Changers* by Richard N. Bolles
- *The Total Money Makeover: A Proven Plan for Financial Fitness* by Dave Ramsey
- *The Life-Changing Magic of Tidying Up: The Japanese Art of Decluttering and Organizing* by Marie Kondo
- *Salt, Fat, Acid, Heat: Mastering the Elements of Good Cooking* by Samin Nosrat
- *Start with Why: How Great Leaders Inspire Everyone to Take Action* by Simon Sinek

Do you notice how the above book titles entice readers *and* offer a promise of improving life in some way?

TITLE STRATEGIES FOR MEMOIR AND NON-PRESCRIPTIVE, NARRATIVE NONFICTION

With non-prescriptive books like memoir, history, social sciences, and philosophy, your approach to developing a title will vary a bit from prescriptive nonfiction. Ideally, your title should accomplish the following:

- Appeal to your ideal target audience. It's essential to keep your niche in mind as you craft your title.

- Describe what the book is about (though in as few words as possible). It's risky to have a brief or non-descriptive title—a tactic that works best for experienced authors who already have a following.

- Be provocative and/or prompt curiosity.

Here are some examples of memorable and captivating titles that work:

- *Man's Search for Meaning* by Viktor E. Frankl

- *Hillbilly Elegy: A Memoir of a Family and Culture in Crisis* by J.D. Vance

- *Eat, Pray, Love: One Woman's Search for Everything Across Italy, India, and Indonesia* by Elizabeth Gilbert

- *Tuesdays with Morrie: An Old Man, A Young Man, and Life's Greatest Lesson* by Mitch Albom

- *Wild: From Lost to Found on the Pacific Crest Trail* by Cheryl Strayed

- *The Happiness Project: Or, Why I Spent a Year Trying to Sing in the Morning, Clean My Closets, Fight Right, Read Aristotle, and Generally Have More Fun* by Gretchen Rubin

- *Furiously Happy: A Funny Book About Horrible Things* by Jenny Lawson

- *Unbroken: A World War II Story of Survival, Resilience, and Redemption* by Laura Hillenbrand

- *The Age of Gold: The California Gold Rush and the New American Dream* by H.W. Brands

- *Chicken Soup for the Soul: 101 Stories to Open the Heart and Rekindle the Spirit* by Jack Canfield and Mark Victor Hansen

- *Women in Science: 50 Fearless Pioneers Who Changed the World* by Rachel Ignotofsky

- *The Rise and Fall of the Dinosaurs: A New History of a Lost World* by Steve Brusatte

- *Travels Through the French Riviera: An Artist's Guide to the Storied Coastline, from Menton To Saint-Tropez* by Virginia Johnson

- *Enlightenment Now: The Case for Reason, Science, Humanism, and Progress* by Steven Pinker

- *A Whole New Mind: Why Right-Brainers Will Rule the Future* by Daniel H. Pink

- *The Power of Habit: Why We Do What We Do in Life and Business* by Charles Duhigg

- *How to Win Friends and Influence People: The Only Book You Need to Lead You to Success* by Dale Carnegie

RESEARCH YOUR TITLE

Before you settle on a title, make sure it isn't part of a registered trademark and that it's not in use by another author. While a book title cannot be copyright protected and can therefore be used by more than one author, if the title is part of a registered trademark for a business name or process, then it cannot be used for your book title. We cover more on this in Chapter 8.

Visit the United States Patent and Trademark office to search for your title in the trademark database: uspto.gov/trademarks-application-process/search-trademark-database.

Also search Amazon and Google with your title in quotes like this: "My Awesome Book Title." This will show you any exact matches for the title/phrase you search for. If you find a book with the same title, we recommend making a change. While titles can legally be duplicated, it can potentially confuse readers and just look unprofessional to use one that has already been published.

Don't forget to search for your subtitle, too. It can be costly to realize you've made this mistake unknowingly after the book is released.

WRITE YOUR JACKET COPY

The back cover is where you convince readers to buy. One trick that many writers use is to craft a compelling description before writing the manuscript because it can help to know what to focus on when developing the manuscript. You have a very limited amount of space on the back of your book so every word counts. The ultimate goal is to entice your target audience and convince them to purchase your book. With this in mind, here are some guidelines:

Research Other Books – Start by reading the jacket copy on other books, especially from books in the same genre as yours. Find out how other authors position their books and what benefits they highlight. This will help you get a better understanding of what jacket copy should look like. It can also help you identify ways that your book is different from your competitors, which you'll want to emphasize when writing your copy. You can also do much of this research on Amazon since most book listings feature the back-cover copy or an expanded version of the back-cover copy.

Start Writing – Write a compelling, and brief, opening paragraph. Draw readers in by identifying them directly, and then help them relate to the solutions offered by your book. Starting with a question can also help readers relate.

Here are some real-world examples:

"Advances in behavioral sciences are giving us an ever better understanding of how our brains work, why we make the choices we do, and what it takes for us to be at our best. But it has not always been easy to see how to apply these insights in the real world—until now."
   —*How to Have a Good Day: Harness the Power of Behavioral Science to Transform Your Working Life* by Caroline Webb

"Anarchy is coming. Decentralization is accelerating, and technology is facilitating the trend. Nobody trusts traditional institutions or authority figures anymore. Bitcoin, open source, Uber, social media and the Arab Spring are all examples of anarchy in action. Tomorrow's leaders need to understand these trends if they wish to thrive in a decentralized economy."
   —*Anarchy, Inc.: Profiting in a Decentralized World with Artificial Intelligence and Blockchain* by Patrick Schwerdtfeger

"Do you feel frustrated because you can't seem to finish every item on your daily to-do lists? Do you feel discouraged because you're not effectively managing your workload and responsibilities at your office and home? If so, it's not your fault."
   —*To-Do List Formula: A Stress-Free Guide to Creating To-Do Lists that Work!* by Damon Zahariades

For narrative nonfiction, the jacket copy needs to captivate readers:

"Is it possible for humans to discover the key to happiness through a bigger-than-life, bad-boy dog? Just ask the Grogans."
   —*Marley & Me: Life and Love with the World's Worst Dog* by John Grogan

"Candy Montgomery and Betty Gore had a lot in common: They sang together in the Methodist church choir, their daughters were best friends, and their husbands had good jobs working for technology companies in the north Dallas suburbs known as Silicon Prairie. But beneath the placid surface of their seemingly perfect lives, both women simmered with unspoken frustrations and unanswered desires."

—*Evidence of Love: A True Story of Passion and Death in the Suburbs* by John Bloom and Jim Atkinson

"Which is more dangerous, a gun or a swimming pool? What do schoolteachers and sumo wrestlers have in common? Why do drug dealers still live with their moms? How much do parents really matter? How did the legalization of abortion affect the rate of violent crime? These may not sound like typical questions for an economist to ask. But Steven D. Levitt is not a typical economist. He is a much-heralded scholar who studies the riddles of everyday life—from cheating and crime to sports and child-rearing—and whose conclusions turn conventional wisdom on its head."

—*Freakonomics: A Rogue Economist Explores the Hidden Side of Everything* by Steven D. Levitt and Stephen J. Dubner

Focus on Benefits – For prescriptive nonfiction, you should highlight benefits that the reader will enjoy, ideally in a bulleted list following the introductory paragraph. To uncover the benefits in your book, identify what problems your book solves for readers. If you wrote a time management book, your benefits might look like this:

Time Management Mastery will teach you how to:

- Reclaim two hours from each and every day (without getting up earlier!).

- Empty that inbox once and for all—and keep it under control forever.

- Improve your productivity by 500% with one simple change.

- Reduce your stress by starting a simple daily habit.

Note how each item above promises to improve the reader's life in some way. This is a basic sales technique when convincing someone to buy just about any product, service or book.

For narrative nonfiction, you may not overtly list the reader benefits, but you still need to think about what's in it for the reader. Ask yourself these questions:

- How will the reader be entertained?

- What will the reader learn as a result of my story?

- What kind of journey will the reader be taken on?

The jacket copy for Jeannette Walls' *Glass Castle,* a memoir that spent over seven years on the *New York Times* Best Sellers list, hooks the reader by answering the questions above. See for yourself:

> *The Glass Castle* is a remarkable memoir of resilience and redemption, and a revelatory look into a family at once deeply dysfunctional and uniquely vibrant. When sober, Jeannette's brilliant and charismatic father captured his children's imagination, teaching them physics, geology, and how to embrace life fearlessly. But when he drank, he was dishonest and destructive. Her mother was a free spirit who abhorred the idea of domesticity and didn't want the responsibility of raising a family.
>
> The Walls children learned to take care of themselves. They fed, clothed, and protected one another, and eventually found their way to New York. Their parents followed them, choosing to be homeless even as their children prospered.
>
> *The Glass Castle* is truly astonishing—a memoir permeated by the intense love of a peculiar but loyal family.

Walls' description is enticing and relatable—anyone who has ever been part of a dysfunctional family will likely relate. It also promises to be hopeful, so that the reader will be inspired. This is the magic formula needed to make truly great jacket copy.

End with a Call to Action – After your list of benefits or your compelling description, wrap up your copy with a strong call to action. That means that you are going to ask the reader for the sale (the gentle art of persuasion). Here are some examples:

- If you're ready to take back control of your life, you need this book!

- Never before has anyone revealed so many inside secrets to the industry. Can you afford not to buy this book?

- This book will show you exactly what it takes to lose 10 pounds in 30 days—so don't waste another moment!

- Don't miss this opportunity to learn the proven system to make more money while working fewer hours. This book will change your life!

For historical books, memoir, and narrative nonfiction, your call to action will be subtle. In the example above from Jeannette Walls, the final sentence draws in the reader, with the goal of making her want to buy the book:

> *The Glass Castle* is truly astonishing—a memoir permeated by the intense love of a peculiar but loyal family.

If this is your first time writing sales copy, you may want to hire a copywriter or an experienced editor to review your work and offer suggestions for improvement. The sales copy for your book can have a *huge impact* on a potential reader's decision to buy your book or move on to something else. Make sure your copy reflects the best your book has to offer.

Write Your Author Bio – The bottom of your back cover should include a brief author bio, and it should consist of highlights from your career or life *as it pertains to the book*. This is not the place to mention pets or hobbies (unless you're being humorous or it relates to the book in some way). Instead, focus on your biggest accomplishments including the number of years of work history you have in the field related to your book, special credentials, major media outlets where you have been featured, awards you've won, and anything else that demonstrates your authority in your field. Don't forget to include your website link and a professional headshot of you.

ORGANIZE YOUR RESEARCH

Incorporating research into your book can improve the manuscript, but it can also slow down the writing process, so it's important to be organized. Gretchen Rubin, *New York Times* bestselling author of *The Happiness Project* and *The Four Tendencies,* served as the opening keynote speaker for the 2018 Nonfiction Writers Conference and shared her process for organizing research:

"I always do my books the same way—I start with a gigantic amount of notes. So, I'll just get interested in something and I'll just take notes and it will all be in one document, one gigantic document. And I find my way around by just using search. Like if I want to find everything having to do with accountability I'll just put the word *accountability* next to it so I know I can find it."

If you include studies or quotes in your manuscript, but you still need to go back to the source material to get the actual information, one trick is to make a note in the manuscript so you know to come back later and fill in the missing information. This keeps the flow of writing going so that you can focus on getting words on paper and avoid worrying about research, looking up websites, and other tasks that destroy the flow of the writing process.

When Stephanie is writing, she notes a simple "XXX" to mark places in her manuscript that need additional research, verification, or details to be added. Later, she can set aside time specifically for those research tasks and easily search for those notations.

CITING SOURCES IN YOUR MANUSCRIPT

There are some general style guidelines to follow when citing sources in a book. Most writers and editors in the publishing industry use and recommend the *Chicago Manual of Style* (chicagomanualofstyle.org). You used to have to buy a big manual to reference, but thanks to modern technology, you can use their subscription-based service online, with a 30-day free trial to get started.

Scholarly writers, or those in the academic realm, follow industry-specific style guidelines. For example, APA style is defined by the American Psychological Association, and MLA style is defined by the Modern Language Association of America. If you work in a specialized field, you may want to see if there are standard style guidelines to follow.

Some Basics to Follow:

- Titles of books, print publications, and reports are typically italicized in in-text citations.

- Put titles of articles in quotation marks.

- Be sure to include the author's (or authors') first and last name(s), source title, and publication year.

- If your work is more scholarly in nature, include the page number(s) on which your quoted text appears.

Following are several formatting options. Whichever style you choose, be sure to use it consistently throughout your manuscript.

Option 1: Simple In-Text Citation

With this format, simply state the author and date—or author, publication name, and publication date—in parentheses directly after the quote or incorporate details as part of your text. There are typically no endnotes for these citations, but if you have a substantial number of quotes, you may want to include a complete list of cited works at the end of your book.

Example:

"If you are not afraid of the voices inside you, you will not fear the critics outside you" (Natalie Goldberg, *Writing Down the Bones: Freeing the Writer Within,* 2nd edition, Shambhala 2005).

Another way to handle this citation:

According to Natalie Goldberg, author of *Writing Down the Bones: Freeing the Writer Within* (2nd edition, Shambhala 2005), "If you are not afraid of the voices inside you, you will not fear the critics outside you."

This can get rather cumbersome, so if your text includes a lot of citations, we recommend compiling endnotes.

Option 2: Endnotes

Endnotes, which are sources cited at the end of the chapter or book, are a more efficient way to cite your sources. To utilize this option, place superscripted numbers (in chronological order) after a quote, followed by a Notes page that you insert at the end of the chapter or end of the book. Here's an example of how it would appear in the text:

"Each year, thousands of people quit their jobs, sell all of their belongings, and move away to a private island to live a life of simplicity."[1]

Then, for each of your sources, insert an entry that will appear in your Notes section at the end of the chapter or book. Entries look similar to those in the in-text version, and at a minimum should include the author, publication name, and publication date.

Here's an example of the cited source from the example above:

1. Annie Author, *Quit Your Soul-Sucking Job and Retire to Island Life for Good*, (New York, Oh-So-Random House Publishing, 2018)

Make sure the order of the sources on the Notes page follows the order the sources appear in the book.

For a more in-depth look at how to cite specific types of publications, visit chicagomanualofstyle.org/tools_citationguide.html.

PRO TIP: *Find the proper citation.*

If you need help locating sources, Citation Machine is a website where you can type in the book details and it will come up with a citation for you: citationmachine.net.

DEVELOP AN OUTLINE

An outline is an essential tool to organize your writing and ensure the content of your book flows well. Think of it like driving a car to a destination you've never been before. You might have a general sense of where you're headed and which freeways you should take, but you would avoid mistakes and get there much faster by following a detailed map. Your outline is the map that helps get your manuscript to its final destination.

There are a number of ways to develop an outline. The most basic is the way you learned in school. Just write one as best you can and use it to help form the table of contents for your manuscript. While this may work for some, we recommend investing time and energy into developing an in-depth outline for your entire manuscript so you don't lose focus as you write.

The storyboard method is one of our favorite strategies and may work well for you, too. Start with a stack of 3 x 5 cards or sticky notes and write down every single topic idea for your book, large or small, until you've emptied all ideas out of your head (and out of any notes you've been keeping). Think of it like a giant brain-dump session, and capture every single detail you want to cover. This process might be completed in an afternoon, or you may want to spend a few days or even weeks on it if needed.

Next, begin to organize your notes in a logical order. This might require a large table or even a big space on the floor so you can spread them all out. The goal here is to separate them into chapters, from the beginning to the end of the manuscript. This will allow you to see where you may have bulky chapters that need to be split in two, where chapters may need to be expanded, and how the overall flow of your content will work.

An outline is just a starting point. You don't have to follow it exactly, and it can absolutely change and evolve as you write. However, an outline gives you the map you need to traverse your writing journey without taking too many detours.

CREATE THE TABLE OF CONTENTS

Whether you use the storyboard method or create a traditional outline, the outline becomes the foundation for your table of contents. The content should include the larger elements of your book such as the introduction, chapters with titles, acknowledgments, appendix, etc., and may not be as detailed as the outline you work from as you write.

 PRO TIP: *Manage your table of contents.*

Keep your table of contents in a separate document titled "TOC." This way you can easily modify it as you write. Then, once you're done with the manuscript and it's fully edited, you can copy and paste it back into your main document. You don't need to worry about assigning page numbers or linking the table of contents to pages since page numbers will change when the interior of the book is typeset.

LEVERAGE CONTENT YOU ALREADY HAVE

Many nonfiction writers incorporate content from previous projects into a manuscript. This means that your book may already be further along than you realize. If you've written content for your website or business, you may be able to use it for your book. Here are some places to look:

- Articles and blog posts you've written

- Handouts you developed

- Surveys you conducted

- Case studies and client success stories

- Seminars, videos, and recordings that can be transcribed

- Contributions from others (articles, interviews, case studies, etc.—with their permission, of course)

- Content you've contributed to other blogs, magazines, newsletters, and websites

If you contributed articles to other publications, make sure to confirm that you have the right to repurpose that content in your book. Many larger publications require copyright control over the works they publish, which may have been implied when your article was published. If that's the case, you can request permission for rights back to your work—and you may receive permission with the caveat that you give credit to the publication where the article first appeared.

Starting with content you previously wrote can help you get a jumpstart on your manuscript. Copy and paste content into your manuscript document, in the appropriate chapter sections according to the outline you created. You should modify the content to fit the tone and flow of your book.

If you're still in the process of thinking about writing your first book, or you plan to write additional books in the future, consider how you could start writing blog content now that can eventually be repurposed for your book. This can help you build up an online following while taking steps toward completing your next book.

Don't worry about others seeing the content before it's published. It's valuable to capture the attention of readers on your blog and build anticipation for your future book. Very few people will ever want to read your blog from start to finish, so they will be glad to have the opportunity to buy your book—even if every bit of it was previously posted on your blog. Really!

BEGIN THE WRITING PROCESS

Once you know what topics to cover and you've crafted an outline to chart your course, you are ready to begin writing. To make the writing process feel less overwhelming, tackle it in small pieces. When approaching it bit by bit, it can begin to take shape faster than expected. Here are some ways to manage the writing process:

- Approach each topic as if you are writing a short article. This will help you stay focused on the topic at hand while making it easy for your readers to enjoy.

- Break up text with plenty of sub-headings and bullets. This makes for easier reading, which your readers will appreciate.

- Share stories (real-world or hypothetical examples) and use metaphors to illustrate important points.

- If you get stuck on a topic, move on to something else and return to it later.

- Avoid editing while you write—this can slow you down. Experienced writers are taught to write first and edit later.

- Beware of getting sidetracked. If you stop the writing process to research something online, you can interrupt your flow and lose track of time. Make a note about the added work you need to do and keep writing. Set aside time later to do your research.

- Develop a system for jotting down notes when you need to add more information, look up a resource or conduct any other kind of follow-up. You might mark a spot in the manuscript with "xxx" so that you can easily search and follow up later.

- Include quotes from people you have interviewed, provide resources for additional information, and compile brief sidebar tips to enhance the reader's experience.

- Pack as much value into your book as possible. The best way to gain a fan is to write a book that has impact. Don't be afraid of giving away your trade secrets and best advice. If you fear that readers won't need to hire you as a result of reading your book, think again. You can outline a process step-by-step, just as we're doing with this book, but that doesn't mean readers won't want to hire you to help them execute the process or keep them accountable. Give them your best work and you'll create loyal fans who want to work with you.

- Don't obsess about the length of your manuscript since this can affect the quality of the content you write. Focus on writing for the reader and getting the most important points across. If you need to expand your manuscript later, you can always add case studies, sidebars, statistics, or other data. Sometimes it makes sense to keep it shorter as long as the value is there.

MAKE TIME TO WRITE

One of the biggest excuses aspiring authors make is a lack of time to get a book written. Like anything else in life, if you want it badly enough, you have to find a way to make it happen.

You may want to plan your writing time around when you are most creative. Are you a morning person or a night owl? Perhaps you need to get up an hour earlier or stay up an hour later. It's important to discover your own unique process. Some writers are disciplined and write during a set time each day. Or, they write for a set number of minutes or hours per day. Some schedule one or two days each week for writing. It's your choice.

Here's some good news: the typical 200-page nonfiction book is usually somewhere between 55,000 and 65,000 words. While writing a book may seem like a daunting process, it doesn't have to be. If you write just 1,000 words per day—about three typed pages—you'll have a 60,000-word manuscript in 60 days! That's doable, right?

IDENTIFY A GOAL FOR COMPLETION

Many authors find it helpful to set a target date for completing the manuscript (several months before the book is published) and then a separate target date for completing the book. If you need help with accountability, enlist a friend or coach to help you reach your goals. If you have a big event coming up, such as a conference where you're speaking, this can provide extra motivation to get it done.

TRY THIS: *Set Goals*

Set a goal to write _____ words per day/week.
Set a goal to complete writing your manuscript by:
   (date) _____
Set a goal to have your book published by: (date) _____

BEGIN THE REWRITE PROCESS

After your first draft is complete, go back through your manuscript from beginning to end and fix errors, fill in places that need clarification, and cut out anything that doesn't add to the mission of the book. Most writers re-read and modify their manuscripts several times before enlisting the help of an editor.

WRITE A DEDICATION AND/OR ACKNOWLEDGEMENTS (OPTIONAL)

A dedication is an extremely brief mention of a name or two of someone special to whom the book is dedicated. It is usually found in the opening pages, before the first chapter.

An acknowledgments section is also optional. Acknowledgments can be lengthier and incorporate some of the "practical" people who helped develop your book, such as your partner, children, colleagues, writers who contributed content or research, the editor, formatters, designers, publisher, etc.

WRITE YOUR AUTHOR BIO

You'll likely need a short bio for the back cover or dust jacket flap and a longer bio on the last page of the book (optional, though strongly recommended). If your book is prescriptive, make sure to include professional and/or educational credentials that tell readers what experience you have and why they should trust your advice within.

If your book is a memoir or narrative nonfiction, the details of your author bio can be more personal or even playful. If you've written a memoir about your experiences studying birds in different countries, for example, you could mention what countries you've visited and whether you own any birds yourself.

Here's a real-life example of a well-written author bio that is both informational and entertaining:

Marie de Haan—wife, mother of three, piano teacher, songwriter, and writer—is back again, snarky as ever. *Cancer Is a Funny Thing: Reconstructing My Life* is the heartwarming follow-up to Marie's memoir about her breast cancer diagnosis and details her pursuit of joy and purpose in the midst of continued treatment and healing.

Diagnosed with Stage III breast cancer at the age of 42, Marie was given a poor prognosis. Putting on her big-girl panties, she endured surgery and chemotherapy, albeit kicking and screaming. At visits to the naturopath, the battle continued over her consumption of sugar. In between all of her doctor appointments and infusions, Marie started a cancer blog, which covers such subjects as poop, boobies, and sex.

Now, as if six doctors wasn't enough, she agonizes about adding a plastic surgeon—to perform a breast reconstruction—to the mix, all the while trying to stay on top of medical bills, lose weight, fulfill her dream of meeting Fran Drescher, and accomplish her never-ending to-do list. She handles all of these issues with humor and grace. And Häagen-Dazs Rocky Road ice cream.

Marie de Haan lives near Seattle with her husband and one to three children at any given time. In addition to teaching piano and writing books, she regularly embarrasses herself on her cancer blog.

Drop her a line at cancerisafunnything.com.

A portion of the proceeds from this book will be donated to the care, diagnosis, research, and treatment of breast cancer.

Your bio can also include a pitch for your services, mentions of previous books you've written, that you're available for speaking engagements, or all of the above. Be sure to also ask for a book review. For example: "If you enjoyed this book, the best way to thank me is to post a review on Amazon."

FINALIZE THE BOOK TITLE

You're not alone if you struggle with deciding on the book title. For most of us, book titles change many times before we're ready to go to press. Oftentimes the title comes directly from some text within the book, and it can be something you weren't expecting! When in doubt, reach out to your social media network and ask for help. You might be surprised by how many people chime in to vote on their favorite option from your list of choices.

GET FEEDBACK

Send sample chapters to a few trusted readers for review and feedback. Then make any final changes needed. You may also want to enlist a team of beta readers. We'll address this topic in the next chapter.

DECIDE WHEN YOU'VE ACHIEVED YOUR *LAST* DRAFT

It's not uncommon to struggle with knowing when a manuscript is complete. Just about any writer will tell you that every single time she reviews her work, she is compelled to make changes. At some point you have to just decide the cake is baked and ready to be served.

There is a saying in publishing: "There is no such thing as a *final* draft, only a *last* draft." You could keep editing and adjusting your manuscript for years, or you could get to a point where you simply decide you've had enough and it's ready to go. When you're sick and tired of looking at it, that's usually a pretty good sign that you're about done.

PREPARE YOUR MANUSCRIPT

Once your manuscript is complete and ready for feedback and editing, you'll want to make sure that it's as clean and consistent as possible. Here are some tips for formatting:

- Don't use double spaces after periods. For books, we only use a single space after a period. If you're still in the habit of writing with double spaces, you can do a find and replace to insert a single space after periods.

- Use consistent fonts and paragraph spacing throughout. As a general rule, editors like to review a double-spaced manuscript in 12-point Times New Roman font.

- Set consistent heading and sub-heading sizes throughout.

- Use bullet points and sub-headings to make your book easier to read. In an age of short attention spans, readers appreciate when you break up long amounts of text.

 PRO TIP: *Offer bonus material.*

One great way to drive readers to your website is to offer bonus downloads such as printable checklists, worksheets, lists of resources, quizzes, or other interesting content that makes them want to drop everything and visit your website. Ideally you should have a landing page where readers input their name and email address before downloading the bonus material, and then voilà! You've given your readers an additional bonus to appreciate while building your mailing list. Offer a few bonus items throughout your book to ensure that the majority of your readers participate.

CONGRATULATIONS! IT'S A BOOK!

We've never known any author who wasn't excited about the arrival of a new book. Even after many titles, we are both still excited when a new book is released. It's a lot like a baby, and it usually takes longer than nine months to be born!

Just as with a baby, after the book arrives, you will be plunged into a new world. All of your preparation will have focused around the birth. Now that it's alive in the world, you need to figure out how to take the next steps to make that book successful. Keep reading.

 # AUTHOR INTERVIEW

Name: Claire Cook

Book Titles:
Never Too Late: Your Roadmap to Reinvention (without getting lost along the way)
Shine On: How to Grow Awesome Instead of Old
Must Love Dogs (Bestselling novel turned movie starring Diane Lane and John Cusack. Also a 6-book series.)

Website: ClaireCook.com

Can you tell us about your publishing journey and why you chose to self-publish your book?

I tell the whole story in *Never Too Late,* but in a nutshell, I was cruising along, represented by a powerful literary agent from a mighty agency that I both liked and respected, published by a series of big New York publishers that believed in my books and helped me make them better, and receiving advances for my novels that were substantial enough to live well on.

And then the publishing world began to get rocky, just like the music world and the newspaper world and so many others had before it.

I was one of the lucky authors. I had multi-book contracts, I was still being sent on book tours by my publisher and published in both hardcover and paperback, so I was able to put on my blinders and ignore the changes at first. Eventually, I couldn't help noticing my career stalling out. So, I hired a lawyer and eventually got the rights to my backlist reverted and began publishing my new books myself. I now own and have published/republished 15 of my 18 books.

I'm grateful that my readers stayed with me. They weren't the least bit interested in who published my books—they just wanted to read the next one. And I'm proud to say that I hit the *New York Times* Best Sellers list under my own steam!

What kind of business are you in and how have your books helped to grow your business?

I'm a fulltime author. The overarching theme of all my books, fiction as well as nonfiction, is essentially reinvention. As a novelist, I was often invited to speak and teach, but always as "Claire Cook, bestselling novelist." But writing two nonfiction books has opened up lots of new doors for me in terms of giving keynotes and teaching workshops. In a sense, my nonfiction books have legitimized me as a "reinvention expert."

What have been some book marketing strategies that have generated the best results for you?

What has worked for me is to treat my readers with gratitude and respect. My readers give me the gift of my career, and I never forget that for a minute.

Is there anything you would do differently for your next book? Any hard lessons learned?

With each book, I learn to listen to myself more. It's so easy to fall into the trap of wanting the *experts* to make our decisions for us, but the truth is that we all need to become our own experts. Take it all in, learn, but then listen to your gut and your heart. You know more than you think you do.

What advice would you offer to new authors?

Since I made the jump to self-publishing, I hear from lots of emerging authors asking me if I think they should self-publish. I suggest they ask themselves these questions before deciding:

Do you have a better option?

I now think of my years as a traditionally published author as the best internship ever. I kept my ears open and learned from the pros. I internalized the voices of several fabulous editors and had time to figure out who I am as a writer. If you're just starting out and you can get in the traditional door, it will enhance your skills as well as give you street cred, so my advice would be to go for it. If those doors don't open for you, shake it off and move on to Plan B. As I meet more and more self-published authors who have built their careers from scratch, I'm both humbled and inspired by them, but also really grateful that I didn't have to do it myself.

Have you done your homework?

I spent at least a year and a half researching the self-publishing world before I jumped in, and because things change so quickly, I continue to invest lots of time keeping up. (It helps that I'm fascinated by all the twists and turns!) So, Google everything you can find. Join indie author groups online. Connect. Listen. Learn. The more you know, the better your chances for success.

What do you bring to the table?

At this writing, I own 15 of my 18 books—8 new releases and 7 backlist books. I have 24,000 followers on Twitter, 18,000 on my Facebook author page, and a mailing list of 29,000. I share these numbers not to discourage emerging writers, but to make the point that while writing is first and foremost a quality game, it's also a quantity game. Every time I release a new book, the sales of the other books I own start to increase, too. And my loyal, wonderful readers, the ones I've been collecting, reader by reader, since my swim mom days, essentially give me the gift of my career. If you have one book and no following, it's important to recognize that, while it can absolutely be done, you'll have a steeper climb ahead of you.

Do you have an entrepreneurial spirit?

I love all the new tech skills I've learned, everything from formatting to the ins and outs of uploading books at various vendors. I'm crazy excited that I can now control price and promotion. At every phase of the self-publishing journey, you have to choose whether to spend the time learning the skills you need to do it yourself or to spend the money to hire someone who already has those skills. But even if you hire out, the buck stops with you. I'm tenacious. When I make a mistake, I learn from it and see it as an opportunity to do it right the next time, and best of all, as a self-publisher I have the power to fix it myself. I put on my blinders and rise above all the negativity that's out there, which can sometimes be the biggest challenge of all.

Is it all about the writing for you?

Several books ago, a surprised new editor said to me, "Wow, it's still all about the writing for you, isn't it?" Absolutely. And the day it isn't, the day I've lost that passion, I hope I have the good sense to go find something else I can love just as much as I've loved writing books. I put my heart and soul into every book I write, and I try to become a better writer with each one. My readers know that, to the best of my ability, I will never let them down.

CHAPTER 6
BETA READERS

Beta readers are people whom you grant access to your manuscript ahead of the book release. Beta readers are not required and are a totally optional part of the publishing process, however, they can bring a number of advantages.

There are several goals for beta readers:

- Get early feedback on the content. This can help ensure your manuscript is well-formed and meets the needs of your target audience.

- Enlist editing help. You may want to ask your readers to help point out errors that need to be fixed.

- Build a group of advocates who can help spread the word about the book upon its release.

- Generate book reviews early and quickly.

Guy Kawasaki has spoken at length about how he made his manuscript for his book *APE: Author, Publisher, Entrepreneur,* available to over 250 beta readers. He received editorial feedback and content suggestions that helped improve his manuscript. Then, when the book was released, he had 250 fans ready to write book reviews and help generate word-of-mouth for the book.

HOW MANY BETA READERS DO YOU NEED?

You don't necessarily have to ask beta readers for content feedback, unless that's something you personally want to do. You can potentially run into some frustration when you have too many cooks in the kitchen, so the decision is entirely up to you. In his book *On Writing*, Stephen King said he only allows a few trusted friends to read his manuscripts in advance.

However, beta readers can play an essential role in your book launch by helping to generate reviews and spread the word via social media and their own personal networks. So, whether or not you want feedback on your manuscript, giving early access to it before the book is released can have many benefits.

The goal for every author should be to get your book in the hands of as many readers as possible. And yes, that means giving it to them for free. If each reader tells just five friends about the book, you can earn that "lost sale" back over and over again.

Worried that your manuscript will get shared with people outside of your beta reader community? During the 2017 Nonfiction Writers Conference, Seth Godin addressed this common fear. His response: *"Your problem is not piracy. Your problem is obscurity."* Godin further suggested that authors should give their books away and encourage readers to share them, because the more eyeballs you can get on your book, the bigger your fan base can grow.

Romance novelists use a formula of giving away the first book in a series or selling it at a super-low price (like $.99), in order to get readers hooked on the series. Since romance readers tend to prefer series books, they consume dozens of books each year. So, if you're a new romance author with a three-book series, and you give away the first in the series, that can spark incredible sales for books two and three.

While nonfiction authors don't often write series books, most of us have additional books to offer or related products and services. With this in mind, giving one of your books away can be highly valuable. When you give your book away, you can attract readers to your mailing list, social media, and your other products and services.

Let's say you sell a consulting services package for $2,500. If you gave away your book to 50 prospective clients, at a wholesale cost of about $250 total, and you netted one new client, would it be worth your effort? Imagine you're a speaker who commands $5,000 or $10,000 for a speech. How many books would you be willing to give away in an effort to attract one high-paying speaking gig?

So, whether you give away a book in order to inspire subsequent book sales, or you give it away as a lead generator to bring prospects to your products and services, you can almost always come out ahead. And it costs you nothing to make the manuscript available in PDF format!

This philosophy absolutely applies to generating book reviews and word of mouth. Book reviews influence purchase decisions on Amazon and other retailers. If you had to give away your manuscript to 50 readers in order to generate ten reviews, wouldn't it be worthwhile? Without those reviews, you'd likely generate far fewer book sales. Not to mention that those 50 readers will also quite likely tell others about your book.

The bottom line: enlist the number of beta readers that feels right to you. Maybe you just want 20 or so because this giveaway strategy makes you a little uneasy. That's your prerogative. However, we encourage you to think bigger and consider how much more substantial your book launch can be when you have 100 or more people who are grateful to have had early access to your book, posting reviews and announcing its release to their own audiences.

HOW TO WORK WITH BETA READERS

One of the best ways to organize early readers is to invite them to a private Facebook or LinkedIn group where you can cultivate your community and get them involved in your book-launch process. Ideally you should position participation in your beta reader group as a privilege—an opportunity for people who enjoy your genre to read your new book before the general public. Also note that since not everyone visits online forums regularly, be sure to add them to a private email list so that you can send messages in addition to communicating within the group online.

Once you've added readers to the group, engage with them and show them how to help you. If you're seeking feedback on the manuscript, give them a reasonable deadline to respond. Two to four weeks should be enough.

Also give them guidance about the kind of feedback you're seeking. Do you want them looking for punctuation, spelling and grammatical issues? Do you want them to track changes in Word and send back a red-lined copy? Or do you want them to type up some general feedback? Setting expectations at the beginning can prevent your readers from going rogue and giving you the kind of feedback you don't want.

Speaking of feedback, provide a list of questions you want them to answer. Here are some examples:

- Is there enough level of detail throughout the book or are there areas that need clarification? If so, which areas?

- Were there enough real-world examples or are there areas where additional examples would be helpful?

- Does the content flow in a logical order? If not, how could it be improved?

- What is your overall opinion of the book?

- What would make the book better?

- Are there any concepts or ideas you feel are missing?

The questions shown above could also be incorporated into a document where participants answer these questions for each chapter, if that's the level of feedback you want, though beware of asking them to do too much. You don't want to lose them in the process. Ideally, readers would fill out their answers and return the document to you. You can also create a Dropbox folder where you can share revised versions of the manuscript and where your readers can submit their responses or red-lined copies of the manuscript.

For promotion purposes, you'll also need to guide your readers in how to participate. Make it as easy as possible for them to get involved. Here are some suggestions:

- Make them aware of the book release date.

- Ask them to share via social media and their own email lists.

- Provide them pre-written tweets, memes, book cover images, and content for easy sharing (a private page on your website with details can work just fine).

- Ask them to post reviews on Amazon, BN.com, Goodreads, and more.

- Add incentive by offering a bonus for participation or enter them in a contest to win a gift card or prize of some sort.

- Offer to provide guest posts for their blogs.

Note that Amazon has been scrutinizing reviews, especially those that appear to come from friends of the author. If Amazon deems a review to violate its policies, it can remove the review. It may even ban the user from posting reviews in the future. This is a frustrating policy, though one you should be aware of.

You may want to offer to purchase some copies of your book, print or Kindle editions, to deliver to those who plan to post reviews so that their reviews show up as a "verified purchase," which is noted next to a review. For the Kindle version, you can use the "Buy for Others" option on the book's sales page. You could also ask your readers to buy the book themselves, and then offer to reimburse them.

Remember to maintain regular communication with your beta readers and help them feel involved in your book launch. Let them know the publishing timeline status, thank them for their reviews and shares, and make sure they feel appreciated. You may also want to thank them publicly either in a page in the back of the book, on your website or both.

ENLISTING BETA READERS

In order to make your beta reader program as successful as possible, you'll need to enlist readers. Create a sign-up form on your website for those interested in joining your group. You may want to ask a few questions to screen participants. Here are some sample questions:

- Do you currently enjoy <genre> books? (You want to make sure you're enlisting readers who actually appreciate your genre.)

- Are you interested in providing feedback on the manuscript?

- Are you willing to help promote the book to your own network upon its release?

- Are you willing to post one or more reviews of the book, provided you like what you read? Where will you post them?

- How else will you assist in spreading the word about the book upon its release?

You could also have applicants give links to their own social media profiles and websites, if this is criteria you care about. Having a substantial platform shouldn't be the only criteria to enlist beta readers since it could significantly limit participation, but it can be useful to know how wide their reach can be.

WHERE TO FIND BETA READERS

- Colleagues, peers, clients, past and present co-workers, past and present schoolmates, family, and friends.

- Your own social media networks and mailing list.

- Online groups that reach your target audience. For example, if you're writing a memoir on living with diabetes, locate groups for people who have diabetes.

- Reach out to trade associations, alumni groups, and other professional organizations that reach your target audience and ask them to help you get the word out to their members.

- Goodreads has a public group specifically for finding beta readers (goodreads.com/group/show/50920-beta-reader-group), and so does Facebook (facebook.com/groups/1662819743977604).

- Post to writers' forums and communities, such as Absolute Write, (absolutewrite.com/forums), Writer's Circle (mywriterscircle. com), and The Nonfiction Book Club on Facebook, which is hosted by Stephanie Chandler (facebook.com/groups/ nonfictionbooklovers). Members of the Nonfiction Authors Association can also post invitations to the private member groups on Facebook and LinkedIn.

TIPS FOR A SUCCESSFUL BETA READER PROGRAM

- The beta reader experience shouldn't feel like a one-way transaction where your readers are there only to serve you. When they're appreciated and know that their participation makes a difference, they will feel even more inspired to help spread the word about your book and about you as an author they admire.

- Engage with your beta readers often so you keep them interested and make them feel like they are a valued part of the process.

- Acknowledge your beta readers somehow. You could thank them in a page printed in your book or in a blog post on your website.

- You could take it a step further and offer extra incentive for their participation, such as membership in a program you manage or extra downloadable content. Added incentives never hurt!

- Show your gratitude by thanking them several times. Tell them how they've impacted the book and what it means to you.

 PRO TIP: *Use a tool to manage manuscript distribution.*

Consider using a tool like BookFunnel.com to distribute your manuscript to beta readers. This allows you to make the digital version of your book available in the reader's preferred format, such as Kindle, Nook or iPad reader. A similar service, BetaBooks.co, allows you to share tracked changes and collaborate with your readers.

CHAPTER 7
EDITING ESSENTIALS

Editing is one of the most important elements of a self-published book. Any book, even from a big New York publishing house, will likely have a handful of errors and typos. This is forgivable. But if you have dozens of errors in your book, you risk disappointing readers and losing credibility. Worse, poor editing will ultimately get noted in reader comments on Amazon and beyond.

There are several types of editing: developmental editing, copy editing, and proofreading. Some manuscripts go through all three levels of editing, while others go through one or two levels. At a minimum, your manuscript should go through at least two rounds of editing, which usually includes copy editing and proofreading. The more eyeballs you have on a manuscript, the better, because editing is a human function and mistakes will be made by even the best in the business.

DEVELOPMENTAL EDITING

If you're seeking comprehensive editing and help in shaping your manuscript, you may want to pursue developmental editing. A developmental editor will dig deep into a manuscript and re-work areas that need clarification, sometimes rewriting entire paragraphs of text or offering suggestions for how the author should rewrite. It's an intense and intimate relationship when you work with a developmental editor. Your editor should be someone who understands the topic you're writing about as well as your overall goals for your book.

Developmental editing can be expensive, but definitely worthwhile. If writing doesn't come naturally to you, if English is your second language, or if you simply lack confidence in your writing skills, an experienced developmental editor can polish your manuscript into a masterpiece. Many writers work with developmental editors, including the *New York Times* bestsellers, so know that this is quite common in the industry. It's also the most expensive level of editing because it's labor-intensive, so be prepared for an investment.

COPY EDITING

A copy editor reviews the entire document to make sure all of the formatting and writing structures are correct and work to your greatest advantage. She reads the book to make sure that all the written language is used correctly and that the overall structure is successful in getting your message across. She corrects basic grammar, punctuation, and spelling errors and looks for inconsistencies in the text.

A copy editor does not write your book for you or change your intended message in any way, though she may recommend areas where you need to make your message clearer or stronger. She may point out sections that are confusing and suggest that you clarify what you were trying to say.

The copy (written words) of your book should work to fulfill your goals without drawing attention to itself. *So, for example, a copy editor will point out long, complicated sentences which, although they may be brilliant and enlightening, are, nonetheless, overly complicated and stand out by drawing attention to themselves and away from your primary message, which should, at all times, be the most important part of your book, never allowing other factors, such as your own awkward writing, to get in the way.* (See what we mean?)

In addition to finding and eliminating awkward writing, the copy editor will also look at the book from a higher level to make sure the overall structure makes sense and is consistent. For example, if you say "A, B, and C" in your introduction, then you should use "A, B, and C" throughout the book. You should not sometimes use "B, A, and C" or "C, B, and A."

Traditionally, a copy editor's job consists of The Five C's: Make the copy:

- Clear

- Correct

- Concise

- Complete

- Consistent

In addition, the copy editor ensures that you use the appropriate level of jargon. Every field has its own terminology. If you're writing a book for the general public you'll use a low level of jargon and define things very simply. If you're writing for an audience within a specific field, you can use a much more complicated level of jargon.

Finally, the copy editor will make sure that all tables, illustrations, and other "elements" in your book have appropriate and consistent titles and captions. She will make sure that headers, footers, section headings, chapter titles, and other elements of your book are consistent and always work to advance the look, feel, and message of your book.

Please do not skip over copy editing. It is an essential part of a professionally produced book.

PROOFREADING

The final phase of editing is proofreading, which is a review of the manuscript for simple errors, typos, and mistakes with grammar, punctuation, and spelling that weren't caught during the copy-editing phase. Proofreading is the last step and is meant to polish your manuscript and get it print-ready. Imagine your dentist polishing your teeth after a cleaning. That's what proofreading does for a manuscript.

HIRING EDITORIAL SUPPORT

Editing is a profession. We implore you to *please, please, please hire a professional editor*—someone who edits books for a living. This is extremely important and may make or break the success of your book.

Unfortunately, poor editing is one of the reasons that self-publishing still has some stigma around it, because too many authors skimp on editing and end up with subpar books. Your primary goal as a self-published author is to make your book look like it was produced by a major New York publishing house, and that means that it is thoroughly edited by one or more professionals.

A professional editor is *not* your sister, the high school English teacher, or your cousin who is "a really good writer." Though these people may help you get your manuscript ready for editing, they are not publishing industry professionals. They won't follow a standard style guide like the Chicago Manual of Style. They won't know to look for consistencies like serial commas. Trust us when we say that professional editing is essential and too often undervalued by authors.

Editing is also the most labor-intensive part of the publishing process and will therefore be one of your largest publishing expenses. Some editors charge by the word, others by the page or by the project. For quality copy editing or proofreading, you can expect to spend between $700 and $7,000. Yes, the range varies widely based on the length of your manuscript, how much work is needed, and how much experience your editor has.

Editors expect to offer a sample of their work and will typically edit a few pages or even a whole chapter of your book for free so you can evaluate their work. Edits are typically done in Microsoft Word using the Track Changes feature. The editor will mark up the document and send it back to you, including notes where changes are suggested. The author can then accept or reject changes and address comments during the review process.

TRY THIS

Convinced you don't need editing? Send just one chapter to a professional editor and see what they find. If it comes back clean, then you are good to go. However, chances are high that errors will be found.

WHERE TO FIND EDITORS

- Ask for recommendations through your local writing community or via the Nonfiction Authors Association.

- The Editorial Freelancers Association offers a searchable member directory.

- You may also find qualified editors through Upwork.com, a freelance directory. Be sure to check references and beware of super-low prices by providers in other countries. If your book is written in English, your editor's native language should be English.

PRO TIP: *Don't skimp on this important step.*

1. Hire a professional editor.

2. Hire a professional editor.

3. Hire a professional editor. (You'll thank us later.)

AUTHOR INTERVIEW

Name: Melinda Emerson, AKA "SmallBizLady"

Book Titles:
Become Your Own Boss in 12 Months, 2nd edition
Fix Your Business: A 90-Day Plan to Get Back Your Life and Reduce the Chaos in Your Business

Websites: succeedasyourownboss.com and fixyourbusiness.com

Can you tell us about your publishing journey and why you chose to self-publish your book?

My first book was published by a traditional publisher, Adams Media, which was acquired by Simon and Schuster. That book has done well, and I published a second edition with them in 2015. When I got ready to write my most recent book, *Fix Your Business,* I went back to my publisher and told them what I wanted to do. They were interested, but in order to ink a new book deal with them, they wanted me to change the title. They claimed the title was negative and wouldn't appeal to book buyers. They suggested that I title the book *Grow Your Business* and use *Fix Your Business* in the subtitle.

I disagreed and pushed back, and then they basically said I could do it the way they wanted to or go elsewhere, which is what I did. I never set out to self-publish my book, but this is the reality of the book business. My effort was going to sell every copy anyway, so I may as well do it myself and make a better margin on the book. Especially since I am a marketing expert with a huge online brand. I knew my audience and every single person I shared my book title with loved it. I was on to something and I decided to go for it.

What kind of business are you in and how has your book helped to grow your business?

I am a national small business expert. I also own a consulting company, Quintessence Group, where we focus on helping Fortune 1000 brands target small business customers. Part of the reason why brands partner with my company is that I've built my SmallBizLady brand online and I reach roughly three million entrepreneurs a week. I'm the host of #Smallbizchat, the largest and longest-running gathering for small business owners on Twitter, which has been held every Wednesday from 8pm to 9pm EST since 2009.

I wrote *Fix Your Business* because I wanted to write a book for existing business owners. Thanks to my first book, I was branded a start-up queen. I want to go up-market and help the existing businesses that had started with my help, but now found themselves trapped in a business that is sucking the life out of them.

For years I've received letters, calls, emails, and social media messages from business owners around the world and across the U.S. who needed help. *Fix Your Business* is a way for me to have a new conversation with my audience. I thought about writing this book for years, but first I had to develop a system I could teach to help them actually reinvent their businesses. Along the way I realized that many of them needed to reinvent themselves, too. So, I created the "12 Ps of Running a Successful Business" and wrote *Fix Your Business* to teach the process.

Books give you a reason to get media attention, give keynote speeches, and host online courses and workshops. You cannot be taken seriously as an expert without a book, and it needs to be well-written and actionable.

What have been some book marketing strategies that have generated the best results for you?

With all of my book launches, I hired a publicist to help develop and execute the launch plan. I got started with a publicist a year before the release of my first book. With the second edition and my self-published book, which both went to print faster, I got started six months before the release.

It was very effective to do webinars about the book content and to write blog posts and guest posts about the topics in the book to drive interest. Everyone asks for guest posts these days and no one interviews people anymore, so as you are preparing the media materials, also develop a Q&A in paragraph form about the book, plus five articles that you can offer to media outlets and influencers to post.

Is there anything you would do differently for your next book? Any hard lessons learned?

I would record the audiobook version immediately so that it could be released at the same time as the book and ebook versions.

What advice would you offer to new authors?

Develop a system that you want to teach through your book. In my first book, it was my "Emerson Planning System," which is all about how to transition from employee to entrepreneur. In *Fix Your Business,* the system is my "12 Ps of Running a Business," which lends itself perfectly to a webinar or 12-week course. Having a system will give you so much more to talk about when you do media interviews, and it's perfect for lectures or workshops.

Become a brand before you write a book. Before you publish, you need to cultivate an audience and email list of people who will be interested in reading your book; otherwise, you'll have 500 copies in your garage.

"Everything you've ever wanted is on the other side of fear."

—George Addair

CHAPTER 8
PRE-PRODUCTION FOR SELF-PUBLISHING

Before you have your book typeset and ready for printing, there are several important steps you need to take.

COPYRIGHT REGISTRATION

Every author should protect their work by registering the copyright, and this isn't as complicated as it sounds. First of all, you essentially own your copyright just by claiming it like this:

Copyright © 2018 Karl W. Palachuk

 PRO TIP: *Add the copyright symbol:* ©

To create the copyright symbol in Word, type the letter "C" into parentheses like this: (C). Word will automatically convert it to the symbol.

One of the old myths about copyright protection is that you have to prove that you wrote something, so you should mail a copy to yourself in an envelope so it comes back with a date stamped on it. But these days, with the internet and computers, you've got date stamps all over the place. Once you publicly display your work, you own the copyrights to it. Period.

But then there's the matter of copyright infringement. You *should* (in our opinion) officially copyright your work on the off chance that someone violates your copyright. Having your copyright registered with the U.S. Copyright Office gives you the ability to pursue legal action.

First, you can sue for related "damages," but you cannot sue for *copyright infringement* in a U.S. court without copyright registration. Second, if your work is registered before publication, or within five years of publication, the act of copyright registration is accepted by the courts as prima facie evidence that you are the copyright holder. This means that if you ever go to court, a judgment in your favor is almost automatic.

If copyright registration is made prior to an infringement of the work, statutory damages and attorney's fees will be available to the copyright owner in court actions. Otherwise, only an award of actual damages and profits is available to the copyright owner.

FIVE COPY RIGHTS

If you go to sell (or even protect) your copyright, be aware that there are five exclusive rights within the concept of "copyright." They include the following:

(1) The right to reproduce (make copies) of the work.

(2) The right to license or sell the work to others.

(3) The right to create derivative works from the original works (these include second editions, multiple revisions, translations, sound recordings, etc. and could include a

new book with a lot of similar material, depending on how much you use of the original work).

(4) The right to publicly display the work.

(5) The right to publicly perform the work.

The copyright owner is permitted to sell or license all or only a portion of these rights. Any sale or license you grant to another must be carefully defined. If you simply say, "sell or license the copyright," it could be construed that you have given away all of your rights, including your right to create derivative works (or second editions).

If you want to retain the right to create derivative works (second editions and new books using a lot of the original material), you must either (1) carefully craft your sale or license agreement to make it narrow enough to not include these rights, or (2) reserve these rights to yourself.

Note: Like all legal issues, none of this is important until it's very important! And by the way, we are not attorneys, so be sure to consult with a professional for accurate and up-to-date advice.

Luckily, the Copyright Office is within the Library of Congress, and you can easily complete the online application and submission process for around $50 at copyright.gov.

You may register a copyright online while the book is in manuscript form (not printed) or after the book is printed, though we recommend registering before your book goes to print. Note that your copyright statement should also be included in the copyright page of your book.

A FEW MORE NOTES ON COPYRIGHT

1. You cannot copyright a book title. So, theoretically, you could write a book called *The Grapes of Wrath*. We don't advise using a title that's already been used elsewhere, but the fact is that you can legally give your book that title if you choose to, provided there is no trademark on that phrase.

You also cannot trademark a book title, unless it's part of a series or you instead trademark the business entity or a proprietary process. *Chicken Soup for the Soul®*, for example, cannot be used as a title because it is a registered trademark.

Be aware that you cannot write a book that infringes on someone else's rights, even if they can't copyright the title. They still have rights they can protect. Don't tempt fate. That being said, if you come up with a great title that is not a protected business name but *is* a book title, you can re-use that title. This is primarily a marketing decision you'll have to make.

2. Some written works are in the *public domain,* which means that no one can claim right to them because we all own them. You can reprint works in the public domain. You can't claim them as your own, but you can reprint them and not have to pay the original author or publisher.

For example, you can reprint anything Charles Dickens wrote. If you add something original, like an introduction and supporting text, then you could copyright that specific production of that book and no one could legally copy your version.

This is why you see whole bookshelves full of store-brand reprints of the classics: it costs essentially nothing to produce them. Now you might not have a use for reprinting old, no-longer-copyrighted material. But you should know that it exists and is available as a resource if you need it.

WHAT CONSTITUTES WORK IN THE PUBLIC DOMAIN?

Typically, a work becomes part of the public domain upon the author's death plus 70 years. The public domain also includes:

- All works published in the U.S. before 1923.

- All works published with a copyright notice from 1923 through 1963 without copyright renewal.

- All works published without a copyright notice from 1923 through 1977.

- All works published without a copyright notice from 1978 through March 1, 1989, and without subsequent registration within five years.

UNDERSTANDING COPYRIGHT LAW AS A WRITER

As writers, and therefore artists, we feel we have an obligation to respect copyright law. This means that you cannot reprint or use someone else's work without their permission. For example, you cannot copy an article from another source and post it to your blog or in your book. You can reference it and provide a link to it, but you cannot publish it in part or in full without permission.

This also applies to images, graphics, clipart, and charts. You can't search Google for a picture of a one-eyed goat and publish it on your blog, in your book, in a PowerPoint presentation, or anywhere else without express permission of the copyright holder. In fact, doing so can result in thousands of dollars in legal fees for a single image violation.

Conversely, others cannot reprint your content, images, videos, music, or other intellectual property without your permission.

If you ever discover someone has published a piece of your content to a blog, you should reach out and ask for it to be removed (or ask for proper attribution). Sometimes this can happen because the blog owner simply doesn't understand copyright law, sometimes the blog owner is hoping you won't notice, and occasionally it's malicious. The best way to deal with this is to send a cease and desist letter, which can be done by email. Here's an example:

Greetings <name, if available>,

I noticed you published an article on your blog here: <link>. I wrote that article and own the copyright to the work, and I did not give permission for it to be published. Please remove that content from your site immediately so we can avoid further legal action.

If the content isn't removed promptly, you may want to contact an attorney specializing in intellectual property and have an official cease and desist letter issued. This can get expensive so you'll need to weigh the pros and cons. If it's a site that is based in a country like Nigeria, where U.S. laws are often ignored and are not enforceable, you may just let it go and move on. Most sites like this aren't well-trafficked so it's not always worth the time, energy or expense.

You may run into a similar situation with your book being offered as a free PDF download by a foreign site—something we see periodically. Don't panic; in most cases, these are scammers who don't even have a copy of your book. And if they did, and a reader were to acquire it for free this way, is that a reader you'd really want to acquire anyway? Those sites look spammy to begin with and are rarely worth your energy, unless they are based in a country where you may have some legal recourse.

RESOURCES

Register your copyright: copyright.gov

How to Investigate the Copyright Status of a Work: copyright.gov/circs/circ22.pdf

Project Gutenberg is a directory of books in the public domain: gutenberg.org

ISBN REGISTRATION

Like a snowflake, your book is unique. But as you've just learned, titles aren't copyrighted. For this and many other reasons, each book must have a unique numeric identifier. This is known as an ISBN or International Standard Book Number.

If you want a deep dive on ISBNs, start at isbn.org. You'll quickly find yourself at myidentifiers.com, which is the home for all-things-ISBN in the United States, and it's where you can purchase your own ISBNs.

By the way, each country has a different organization for assigning ISBNs. You must obtain an ISBN for the country in which your writing/publishing business is located.

ISBNs are assigned to publishers. If you receive an ISBN that is "resold" to you or given to you for free by another publisher or your book printer, then your book will be associated with that publisher. If you obtain ISBN numbers yourself, which we *strongly* recommend when self-publishing, then the numbers will always be associated with the publishing company name you choose.

Each book, and each edition, must have a unique identifier. This makes it possible to know exactly which product is being bought, sold, shipped, etc. If you produce a paperback, hardcover, ebook, and audio edition of your book, you'll need a separate ISBN for each version. And if you release a second edition, you'll need a new ISBN for that.

Bowker is the name of the company that manages the ISBN registration services in the U.S. Once you register your publishing company at myidentifiers.com, you will be able to purchase ISBNs from that site. Currently, the cost is $125 for a single ISBN and $295 for a block of ten. We recommend getting a block of ten at a minimum. And if you plan to write and publish additional books in the future, you may want to go with a block of 100 for $575.

At the end of this chapter is a list of items that get (and don't get) ISBNs. An ISBN number can never be reused. Period.

Some printers offer to sell you their ISBNs to put on your book. This is almost always a bad idea. First, it is a sign to everyone in the supply chain that you are an amateur and a self-published author. If you only intend to sell from the website at that printing house, fine. But if you intend to distribute more widely, you need your own ISBN.

ISBN GRAPHICS

You've seen the barcode on the back of just about every book you've ever purchased. Most major retailers require books and other products to have a unique barcode to help with inventory management and sales. A barcode is a coded set of long black and white lines that look something like this:

ISBN 978-0-9763760-0-2

In addition to the 13-digit ISBN number, you can encode the suggested retail price of the product. That little bit appears to the right of the ISBN itself as a smaller numeric barcode.

There are lots of programs for generating these codes as graphics files. If you use one that you found out on the internet, make sure that it produces a high-resolution graphic. A TIFF format is best. You can get the barcode generated when you buy your ISBNs. The ISBN above is in a file called: **Relax Focus Succeed book_978-0-9763760-0-2__001.tif**

Karl could have just called it "978-0-9763760-0-2__001.tif" but he likes the human-readable component. It keeps him from making stupid mistakes.

Note: Some printers, including Lightning Source and its sister company, IngramSpark, give you the option to create a barcode graphic in the template they generate for you when you use their free book-cover template generator. This is a great option. Because it's already embedded in the template they send you, you know it will look great on the book.

If for whatever reason you had your books printed without an ISBN, you can still have a barcode created and have labels made to attach to your books. With luck, you at least left a place on the back of the book to put your ISBN. If you go this route, have the ISBN code printed on coated, glossy labels that won't get scuffed in shipping.

WHAT ISBNS ARE *NOT*

Please note that an ISBN is not a "barcode" as we normally use that term. Strictly speaking, an ISBN is a number. It's the number that represents your book as it winds its way through ordering, shipping, warehousing, and delivery. The graphic we're familiar with is just a barcode that reflects the numeric information.

ISBNs are not the same as UPCs (Universal Product Codes), EANs (European Article Numbers), or any other barcode graphics that exist in the world of retail. Many industries have their own number systems for tracking items. ISBNs are simply the codes used with books.

WHAT GETS AN ISBN?

Many items can use an ISBN if you intend to sell them beyond your own website. For the latest information, see isbn.org.

These items need an ISBN:

- Audiobooks

- Brochures and pamphlets

- Cell phone novels

- Coloring books

- Graphic novels

- Historical documents

- Loose-leaf volumes

- Maps

- Podiobooks

- Puzzle books
- These items are *not* assigned an ISBN:
- Advertising and promotional materials
- Blogs
- Board games
- Calendars
- Clothing
- Coffee mugs and other utensils
- Comic books (because they are serials)
- Compact Discs (CDs and DVDs). (Music or performance CDs are not assigned ISBNs. Meditation CDs that combine music and spoken word are not assigned ISBNs.)
- Digital customized publications
- Electronic advertising/promotional materials
- Electronic newsletters/e-zines
- Electronic schedulers
- Electronic/video games
- Food and medicine
- Greeting cards. (Greeting cards are not assigned ISBNs unless required by the retailer. If assigned, they are assigned by price point rather than design. For example, if several different designs are all sold for the same price, only one ISBN is used.)
- Magazines (see serials)
- Music/performance CDs (see compact discs)
- Online databases, publications subject to frequent update (blogs, etc.)

- Periodicals
- Personal documents, if digitized
- Pictures and photographs
- Playing cards and tarot cards
- Postcards
- Posters and art prints
- Search engines
- Serials (magazines, periodicals, comic books, etc.)
- Sheet music
- Shirts and other apparel
- Stationery items
- Toys, including stuffed animals
- Web-based games

And of course, there are a few things that may get an ISBN under the right circumstances:

- Journals and diaries can be assigned ISBNs when required by retailers.

- Chapters, paragraphs, and other small sections of published text may be assigned ISBNs if they are being sold separately.

- Compact Discs (CDs and DVDs) may be assigned ISBNs if they are spoken word or instructional.

- Flashcards may be assigned an ISBN if they are instructional in nature.

- Software may be assigned an ISBN if it is educational or instructional.

Note that these are not complete lists. If you have something other than a book, please do your research and determine what's appropriate.

ISBN RESOURCES

- ISBN Registration in the United States: myidentifiers.com

- ISBN Registration in Canada: bac-lac.gc.ca

- ISBN Registration in the United Kingdom: nielsenisbnstore.com

LIBRARY OF CONGRESS CONTROL NUMBER

If you're looking for a government agency that actually works really hard to serve the people it is chartered to serve, then you're going to love the Library of Congress. When in doubt, go to loc. gov/publish and you'll be amazed at how thorough the site is. It's easy to understand as well!

Open up the title page of most books that are professionally published and you'll find something called the Cataloging in Publication (CIP) and Catalog Card Number.

These numbers are used by librarians to locate specific Library of Congress (LOC) catalog records in the national databases. They use this information to order catalog cards from the LOC and to order books from commercial suppliers.

The LOC assigns a CIP number *before* the book is published, so that the CIP number can be printed on the title page of the book once it is published. The goal here is to make it easier for book dealers and librarians to buy your book.

Basically, the process consists of these steps:

1. You send an application along with an electronic copy of your book to the LOC.

2. You are assigned a Control Number.

3. The LOC determines the appropriate category, sub-category, Dewey Decimal designation (I'm not kidding here), and LOC catalog number.

4. You (the publisher) receive this information so you can print it on the copyright page.

5. A machine-readable "official" description of your book is distributed to large libraries, bibliographic utilities, and book vendors around the world.

6. You send a copy of your work (book) to the LOC. They verify that all the information is accurate and add some information to the previous electronic record (for example, final page count).

7. LOC updates the book's electronic records with the latest information.

Your LOC catalog card number should appear on the copyright page of your book. If you can manage to include this catalog number in book reviews, it allows subscribers to the LOC catalog service to order books by number and eliminate a search fee. If you plan to sell to libraries, you must have an LOC number.

Please note: A Library of Congress registration and LOC catalog number are not required to sell your book. But they open up some pretty big markets and the process is easy.

NOTES ON THE PROCESS

Once you create a login, you'll go to loc.gov/publish/pcn to actually enter information for your book.

Follow the links to the PCN Application. You'll need to have the following information:

- Title

- Subtitle

- Edition (if appropriate)

- Publisher

- City/State

- Author name for up to three authors

- Editor name for up to three editors

- Approximate number of pages

- If you plan more than one volume, how many additional volumes do you expect?

- Is this a periodical?

- The ISBN for this title. Use the format with dashes: 978-0-9819978-4-1 not 9780981997841.

- Qualifier (hardcover, paperback, diskette, answer book, volume 1, etc.)

- If the paper is acid-free, check the "permanent paper" box. If you don't know this, leave it blank.

- Primary language if other than English.

- Is the book intended for children or young adults?

- Series title, if appropriate.

- Month of publication.

- Email address where the PCN will be sent.

- Your contact information.

Click Submit and wait up to a week to receive an email with your control number. If you have changes to the information you submitted, you need to wait until you have a PCN and then enter a change request. Once you receive a control number, aim to use it in your publicity so that interested booksellers can easily order your book.

At the time of this writing, the LOC is preparing to launch a new program called the PrePub Book Link. This brings the Library's Cataloging in Publication (CIP) and Preassigned Control Number (PCN) programs together in a unified web-based tool and should simplify the process moving forward.

BISAC CODES

The Book Industry Study Group defines and maintains a list of numeric codes used to help identify the categories where books should be shelved. These codes are used by bookstores and libraries to determine placement for books.

Examples:

BIO029000 – BIOGRAPHY & AUTOBIOGRAPHY / Culinary

MED016030 – MEDICAL / Dentistry / Orthodontics

FAM015000 – FAMILY & RELATIONSHIPS / Divorce & Separation

You can list BISAC codes in the copyright page for your book—most books include around three categories. You can also use these codes to tell Amazon and other retailers how to shelve your books (though they can ignore your suggestions, so don't be surprised if they disagree).

Locate BISAC codes here: bisg.org/page/bisacedition.

"*Good things happen to those who hustle.*"

—Source Unknown

CHAPTER 9
BOOK DESIGN AND PRODUCTION

As self-publishers, our goal should always be to produce our books in the most professional way possible. If your book is ever placed side-by-side with a book from a major New York publishing house, it should *not* be obvious which is self-published. Unfortunately, this is where a lot of new self-publishers go wrong. Our goal here is to help you avoid rookie mistakes and produce a book you can be proud of.

COVER DESIGN

One of the biggest mistakes made by first-time self-publishers is to design their own covers or hire an inexpensive provider who lacks experience in book cover design. As you'll soon learn, the cover of your book is probably the most important marketing tool you have. Remember that old saying, "People judge a book by its cover." It's an iconic statement because it's true.

Unless you're a graphic artist, please don't design your own book cover. Even if you are a graphic artist, you need to study book cover design before you jump in. Book cover design is an art in itself, and there are intricacies that non-cover designers can't understand.

For example, when your cover is shrunk down into a tiny graphic on a mobile phone, the title and author name should still be legible. Covers should also be clean and simple without too many graphic elements. Colors should be balanced, and fonts should be prominent.

Books seem so simple because most of the books you've seen have professional designs, and the design doesn't get in the way. It doesn't stand out. It doesn't draw attention to itself. That's exactly the point. A professional cover design is subtle, yet powerful. Go to Amazon and look at the designs of some of the bestsellers. Most are simple, subtle, professional, clean, and powerful.

Try wandering into your local bookstore and looking at your competition. Go determine where your book would be shelved. What's to the left and right of the books in your category? Since you're obviously in the business, which of these books do you already own? Which are you tempted to buy right now? Why does each cover keep your attention? Is it the font? The layout? The description? A picture?

If you have already spent money on a book, that's a very strong argument for its cover design. If you are tempted to spend money on a book, that's another good argument for good cover design.

A prospective reader will spend a few milliseconds looking at a book cover. Maybe one full second. Then the interested party either flips through the book or flips it over and reads the back cover, which is as important, if not more important, than the front cover.

We believe that the back of your book is the most important marketing you have. If someone spends 30 seconds reading your back-cover copy (or reading the book description online), he is seriously considering purchasing your book. That's a lot of pressure put on one little piece of paper, especially since a good chunk of it is dedicated to boring stuff like your ISBN code and publishing company name.

COVER GRAPHICS

If you want to include visual elements on your front cover, such as a picture of a car or a tree or a baby baboon, you'll need to acquire the rights to print the image. If you took the photo yourself, then you already own the rights. Otherwise you'll have to do what most publishers do and purchase a stock photo.

Photo sites often have restrictions on using photos for items that are to be sold for commercial purposes. Some may limit the number of times the photo is printed on your book cover, which could mean you'd have to renew the license, or buy a different kind of license, if you sell more than 10,000 or 20,000 copies. (Let's hope this is an issue you eventually have to be concerned about!) Be sure to check the terms of use for any image that you purchase. Also note that the image must be in a large format and in the highest resolution possible in order to print well on a commercial printer.

Stock images are usually less expensive than you might think and will likely run you just a few dollars. Popular sites for purchasing images for use on your book cover or in the interior of your book are istockphoto.com and 123rf.com.

COVER TEMPLATE AND PRODUCTION VARIABLES

As with many construction projects where buildings are erected, you build a book in stages. When you start out, you really don't know how big it will be, how many pages it will be, or even what size paper you'll print it on.

The cover template is a file your cover designer can use to begin creating your book cover. It divides the file into the three sections: front cover, spine, and back cover. If you're producing a hardcover edition, the file will include inside flaps for the dust jacket. Your cover designer will load this file into whatever program he is using to create your cover (probably Adobe InDesign).

The cover design template is built in stages. First, you have to decide on the dimensions of your book. Most standard paperbacks have a trim size between 5 x 8 and 6 x 9. If you're producing a workbook or cookbook, your trim size might be 8.5 x 11 or larger.

Once you choose your trim size, you can have your graphic designer start working on the book cover design—both front and back. Eventually, you're going to have to figure out a very important piece of information that most non-publishers never think about: the width of the spine. The spine width is determined by the final number of pages in your book. But that's not all!

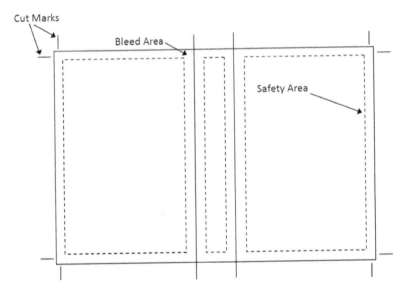

Sample Cover Template

Eventually, you need to create a document that takes all of these things into consideration:

- Front Cover Size
- Spine Size
- Back Cover Size
- Bleeds All Around

As you can see from the sample cover template image, you're going to print an image on a piece of paper. Slightly smaller than that size is the cut size or trim size. This allows you to have images that go all the way to the final edge of the cover.

Inside of the trim lines is a safe printing area. Because printing is not absolutely precise, you need to leave this "bleed" space between the safe printing area and the edge of the final sheet, which is trimmed by the printer to reach its final size. In this manner, you know your design can go to the edge of the safety area.

Here's an outline for a safe process for getting your cover template created. We are using the free cover generator from Lightning Source as an example. This is only one possible printer, and you cannot use their template anywhere else. Each printer will have their own template-generation process. Lightning Source can be found at lightningsource.com/covergenerator.aspx.

1. Decide on your finished book size (see book sizes below).

2. Decide on the paper type (see paper types below).

3. Generate a template with a "wild guess" of the number of pages you'll have.

4. Give this preliminary template to your cover designer so he can start building the design. An experienced cover designer will understand that the spine size will change once the book interior typesetting is complete and you know how wide the spine needs to be.

5. Once you have an exact count of pages, generate the final cover template for your designer.

PRODUCTION VARIABLES

Each printer, whether digital or offset, will have a limited number of standard choices for book trim size. Similarly, they will have some standard paper options, not all of which are available in all book sizes. So, once it's time to start thinking about the actual production and printing, you need to look at four key variables, which drive some other decisions.

1. Binding

Standard paperback books with a spine are called *perfect bound.* This is probably what you thought you'd choose before you knew there were other options. Of course, you can also create a book that's *hardcover* or *case laminate.* If you choose hardcover, you may also choose to print paper dust jacket covers for your book. Depending on your printer, you might be able to print a book that is *cloth bound* or *stitched.*

Because each of these uses a different production process, the paper types and cut sizes will be different for each binding type.

2. Interior Printing: Color vs. Black & White

Unless you have a reason to do so, you will probably print your book with black-on-white interior pages. If you have a cookbook or a photo book, then color is the obvious way to go. You may also simply have a book concept that requires a lot of color.

Color printing costs more, much more than black and white, even with a digital press. And color has other requirements that affect whether the printer will be able to produce books of specific sizes in color. As a general rule, digitally printed books are either all color or all black and white on the inside, which means you can't just insert a few color pages and pay the difference for those. Your book pricing will be based on the whole file being printed in color. This is why black and white printing is the most common option for the majority of books.

3. Book Trim Size

There are many, many size options for books. Here are some very common book sizes:

5 x 8	7 x 10
5.25 x 8	8 x 10
5.5 x 8.5	8.25 x 11
6 x 9	8.268 x 11.693 (A4)
7.50 x 9.25	8.5 x 11

(A4 is the standard letter size in Europe)

This is not a complete list, but it shows some of the most common sizes. Every printer is different, so you'll need to check with yours for a full list of options.

4. Paper Choice

The two most obvious choices for paper are *white* and *cream*. But your printer might have 100 other options. In addition, you may want the paper coated or glossy. Each of these has a different thickness. To most people the difference in thickness is minor and barely noticeable. But when you add up 150 or 200 sheets (300 to 400 pages), the differences in thickness impact the spine size and the weight of the book (which can increase your shipping costs).

As you can see, all of these variables work together to determine the final size of your book. For printers who only print "custom" books and don't have a mass-production template process, you'll need to calculate the book thickness with a formula they give you. And your graphic designer will need to generate his own book cover template.

Once you know the binding type, whether the inside is black and white or color, the final trim size, and the type of paper you're using, you can finally figure out exactly how wide the spine will be. Then you can generate the template and design your book cover.

WHERE TO FIND BOOK COVER DESIGNERS

Please, please, please do NOT hire a cover designer on Fiverr.com. This is a directory for inexpensive freelancers and is better used for simple graphic design projects such as social media headers or internet ad graphics. We cannot emphasize enough how important it is to work with a professional book cover designer—someone who designs book covers *for a living*.

To find a designer, start by asking around in your author community for recommendations or via the Nonfiction Authors Association. Before you hire any designer, be sure to look at a portfolio of their work and make sure you like their style.

You can also hire designers through Upwork.com, a directory of freelancers who are rated by users. Again, be sure to look at a portfolio of work. Another option is 99designs.com, where you can host a contest and allow many designers to submit design concepts for consideration. Then you can award the "prize" (payment) to the design you like best.

INTERIOR LAYOUT/TYPESETTING

Creating the interior layout of your book, also known as type-setting, is an important design element that is typically handled by a graphic designer different from your cover designer. Cover design and interior typesetting rely on two entirely different skill sets, which is why you'll usually need to hire two different designers to handle these tasks.

While you can find instructions online for typesetting your own book, this is another task that is often best left to a professional, provided you can afford to hire it out. Trying to format a printable book in Word is bound to cause headaches since Word isn't designed to handle projects with this level of complexity. A graphic designer imports a final Word document into graphic design software, such as Adobe InDesign, and deals with pagination, headers on the left and right pages, and other design elements.

Here are some tips for interior design:

- For the main text in the book, use a standard Serif font such as:

  - Palatino Linotype

  - Garamond

  - Baskerville

  - Century Schoolbook

  - Times New Roman

    Studies show that these fonts are easier to read, and they're also a standard in the publishing industry. Publishing an entire book in non-serif-style fonts can look amateurish; however, you can use different style fonts for headings and sub-headings to add decorative appeal.

- Avoid using too many font styles throughout the book as it can make a book look chaotic.

- Standard fonts are generally part of the public domain, but if you want to use any specialized fonts for your headings or other parts of your book, you may need to purchase the right to use the font. Providers include fontshop.com and myfonts.com.

- The book should open with a simple title page (title and author's name). Testimonials may also be used as an opening page, followed by a title page.

- A copyright page should be inserted on the back side of the title page.

- The table of contents should be finalized once the book pages are proofed and approved. Page numbers will need to be verified after the interior is typeset.

- After the table of contents, you may have a dedication, acknowledgments, and/or foreword. All of these are entirely optional.

- Page numbers for a book can be on the outside left on left-side pages and the outside right on right-side pages. It is also acceptable to center numbers on the page (which can make it easier to ensure that everything is aligned properly).

- The standard for the top of a page is book title on the top of all left pages and chapter title on the top of right pages.

- Review the file standards for the printer you choose to understand margins and bleed requirements.

A professional book typesetter has to be detail-oriented to ensure that the book is consistent, spacing is accurate, headings are uniform, chapters start on the right side, and images are placed properly. To find a typesetter, ask around in your writing community or via the Nonfiction Authors Association. You may also find a qualified freelancer via Upwork.com.

 PRO TIP: *Fill blank pages.*

Plan for something to place on blank pages. When chapters begin on the right, you will likely end up with several blank pages throughout the book. While it's fine to leave blank pages as-is, take advantage of this real estate by adding in a quick tips, inspiring quotes, interesting facts, images, cartoons, or other short content. Provide your typesetter with a list of blank page fillers.

PROFESSIONAL INDEXING

Before you go to the trouble of indexing your book, you should consider whether it will add to the value of the book. For medical guides, history books, academic manuals, and other books that cite lots of sources and data, an index often makes sense. Librarians also like books with indexes, so if you plan to target the library market, an index can help you make sales. For many books, however, like a memoir or a simple how-to guide, an index may not be necessary.

Indexing takes some effort. Even if you do it yourself, which we don't necessarily recommend, it is more complicated than just running a software program against your text. Generally, indexing starts with a list of every word in your book. Then you remove the most common words (*a, if, the, and, but, with, etc.*) until you have a list of relevant words. You'll need to remove thousands of irrelevant words, so you can see why software helps.

But software doesn't know when two different phrases refer to the same topic, or which technical jargon is important. So, you, as the subject matter expert, need to cull through this list, combining some keywords and deleting others. Eventually you'll come up with a list of the words you really want to index.

At this point, you need to have the book interior typeset exactly as it will appear in print. You'll create a PDF file as if for publication. Now you can run your software against the PDF and go get some coffee as it chugs away.

The software will need to find every occurrence of every word on your list and create a final list of words with their associated page numbers. The output is a first draft of your index, and you'll need to read through it to ensure it makes sense. For example, if you have only one instance of a specific word, do you want to keep it in the index?

Note that once you create the index, you cannot make any changes that would repaginate the book. If you do that, all the page numbers in your index will be wrong and will have to be recalculated. Also note that a revised, updated, second edition will also need to be re-indexed. So, creating a first edition with an index pretty much obligates you to index future editions.

In the end, you need to look at your table of contents and your specific subject matter to determine whether you need an index. Not all books need to be indexed. As with every other layout decision, if it adds value to the book, then do it. If it doesn't add value, don't worry about it.

If an index is important to you, you will save yourself a lot of time and heartache by outsourcing this task to a professional indexer. Yes, this is a professional field where freelance indexers do nothing but create indexes using a combination of software and human intervention. On average, you can expect it pay between $3 and $5 per index-able page. You can locate freelancers through The American Society for Indexing: asindexing.org/find-an-indexer.

GRAPHICS

The first rule of graphics is that you have to start out with really high resolution, meaning 300 DPI (dots per inch) or greater. If you're planning to scan in photos, for example, your standard home printer may not do the best job. Instead, take them to a local Fed Ex/Kinkos or UPS Store and have them professionally scanned. This typically costs around $5 per image.

Also consider how images will be re-sized when placed in a book. If you've developed intricate spreadsheets or charts that are legible in 8.5 x 11 format, be sure they will still be legible when placed in a 6 x 9 format. Otherwise you risk frustrating your readers.

Unless you have a reason to print color graphics on the inside of your book (for example, a coffee table book), you will be using black and white and grayscale on the interior. You'll need to work with a graphic artist to either convert color graphics to grayscale or determine that they look great in grayscale and don't need to be converted.

As previously mentioned, images are also protected by copyright law so you cannot reprint an image you find on Google or anywhere else without written permission from the copyright holder. Your best bet is to supply your own images or purchase images from a site like istockphoto.com or 123rf.com.

You may want to purchase simple line art to add some flair to chapter headings, call-out boxes, or special sections within the text. Graphics are generally good for a book. For many subjects they are necessary. At a minimum, they can add visual appeal and break up the text. So, the message is to use graphics but use them sparingly. Use them to contribute to the overall layout design. Just don't let them detract from your message.

PDFS

PDF stands for Portable Document Format, a layout standard originally designed by Adobe Systems. It is now an open standard, meaning that lots of other companies are designing software around this format.

The PDF standard was designed so that you could exchange documents between computers using different hardware, different operating systems, and different software, and it would always look the same. This means that if you open a PDF on a PC, Mac, or iPad, it will look the same on each device.

Each PDF document contains all the data needed to recreate two-dimensional graphics, text, and fonts. This is a universally successful file format and virtually any printer you send your book to will insist on your book cover and interior files each arriving in a PDF document. Along with your PDF documents, you'll need to send all the fonts and the high-resolution graphics you used.

To save yourself some time, store a copy of your fonts and graphics with your book documents so that you will have them handy when you need to send them to the printer. With many printers, you can send a file with the fonts embedded. That means that all the information needed to reconstruct your fonts will be built into the PDF file. This is handy, *but you have to know how to do it.* The process is different in different programs, so you'll have to make sure your designers (or whoever creates the files) know what to do.

Bottom line: Use Adobe Acrobat (sometimes called Acrobat Writer or Acrobat Professional to distinguish it from the free program Adobe Acrobat Reader). Adobe Acrobat created the standard everyone else emulates. If you use this program, your documents will be consistently correct.

Yes, it's an investment—around $100 outright or $15 per month. But if you buy a cheaper program to create the PDFs, you will likely have problems and end up buying the Adobe product anyway.

Second, you need to embed your fonts and graphics. The printer is not going to keep track of dozens (or hundreds) of files to make sure your graphics and font files are available at the time of printing. So, the PDF format allows you to embed these elements inside the one document.

To embed these elements, you simply need to put them all together in one place and check the right boxes inside Adobe Acrobat when you create the file. If you don't embed the fonts in a PDF file, the local computer that displays it will substitute a close font. That's fine for a couple of pages, although it might display a little strangely. But that can be a disaster in a 300-page book.

Most printers will simply reject your files if the fonts are not embedded or the graphics are low resolution. This is yet another reason you should consider hiring the design tasks out.

PRICING FOR NONFICTION

How much is a book worth? Like everything else, that depends on what people are willing to pay. College textbooks are regularly over $100 each. With a Kindle reader you can download amazing collections of the greatest books ever written, sometimes for free.

Karl's first book was about 100 pages and sold for $89.95. Even though many copies were sold at discounts as low as $69.95, thousands sold at full price. That book is out of print now, waiting for an update. But the ebook version still sells for $79.95 every month.

How can he charge this much? It's simple: he has a niche target audience and a product people want. They use it to improve their businesses. The book costs readers, who are owners of IT companies, less than one hour of billable labor. So, to the buyers, the price is worthwhile.

NONFICTION ADVANTAGES

When it comes to pricing your book, nonfiction has many advantages. Nonfiction books are used to adopt a hobby, understand ourselves, improve our quality of life, learn something new, get inspired, and do a job better. They aren't just books; they're tools.

One mistake some nonfiction writers make is to set the retail price too low. A low price can mean low value in the eyes of the reader. If you have a valuable resource to offer, you need to charge for it. If someone wants a discount, you can give one. But you can never raise the price.

We urge you to resist "cheap" pricing as much as possible. This is especially true if you have a valuable resource for people in a niche industry. If you want to give away copies, do so. But the ones you sell should sell for a good price. People tend to undervalue their own work. Don't be one of them!

STANDARD PRICING

To the extent that there is any standard pricing, here's how you can figure out what it is. Go visit a bookstore or look on Amazon. Find the section where your book should be shelved (you should do this anyway during the design phase to get ideas about size, shape, color, etc.). Pick up the books in that section and look at the prices.

Karl is in the computer business. Almost nothing in his space is under $50. The "sweet spot" is probably $49.95 to $59.95. That's MSRP (manufacturer's suggested retail price). Actual prices are frequently 10% cheaper. But in the computer section, the books are rarely discounted. So, the price is the price.

The same is true for other niche markets. Dr. Ann Marie Gorczyca is an orthodontist who authors books for the dental market, helping dentists to grow their practices. Her 6x9 hardcover books, that average around 200 to 250 pages, retail for $39.95.

Professional books for attorneys, doctors, and medical professionals are typically priced over $30. This is why it's critical that you do the research and see what others in your field are charging for their books.

For more common nonfiction books, including business, self-development, and other how-to books, typical prices for a trade paperback will range between $15 and $19.99. If your book is over 55,000 words or 200 pages, you should probably price it at or near $19.99. This price also makes it easy to collect twenty-dollar bills at speaking engagements, where you announce, "I'll pay the sales tax!"

If your book is shorter, you may be better off pricing it around $15. If you price a 100-page book at $20, be aware that some reviewers may complain. However, you can make it clear in either the book title or description so readers don't feel bamboozled: "This *short* guide to big profits . . ."

Hardcover books command higher prices because they are much more expensive to print, often twice the cost of a paperback. Some professional authors want to offer both a paperback and a hardcover for their executive-level clients, which is totally acceptable. But plan to sell your paperback for around $20 and your hardcover as high as $35.

If you're using your book to build your consulting or speaking business and plan to send copies to prospective clients, a hardcover can impress—especially with a retail price tag of $35. But a paperback can help you reach the masses. In this case, we recommend printing a "special edition" hardcover in addition to the paperback so that you can offer both versions.

Workbooks can be priced in the range of $30 to $60, depending on your industry. There are many authors who sell $40 workbooks to accompany their $20 paperbacks. And if you want to make money upselling books, create a companion workbook to bundle with your trade paperback and watch your sales soar.

For memoir, narrative, and non-prescriptive nonfiction, your price will likely be moderate and under $20 for a paperback. It's important to research your competition so your book is priced within range for your genre.

DISCOUNT PRESSURE

Amazon is the 800-pound, poorly mannered gorilla in the book business. Amazon wants publishers to give it a 55% discount off the retail price. So, if your book retails for $20, Amazon will pay you 45% of the retail price: $9. Deduct your wholesale cost to print the book—around $5—and what's left is your royalty earned: $4. With shipping, you might not break even.

The standard in the brick-and-mortar bookstore world used to be a 40% discount, but thanks to Amazon, many retail stores now expect a 50% to 55% discount. This is an important factor when pricing your book because you need to do the math and make sure you leave enough room to earn a profit. This can be especially challenging for full-color books and hardcovers, which cost so much more to print.

The bottom line is to be reasonable, but don't be shy about pricing your book on the high end of reasonable. When in doubt, start high. You can always bring the price down. But you'll never be able to charge more than the price printed on the cover.

Download our free book pricing calculator here: nonfiction-authorsassociation.com/reader-bonus.

ONSITE SALES AND DISCOUNTS

When you give speeches, you might be tempted to sell your books at a discount. Since Amazon may be discounting your book, you might think that your audience wants to get it cheaper online—and they certainly could. But don't undervalue instant gratification. When you've just dazzled a room of prospective readers, they will want to take a piece of you home with them. Why wouldn't they pay full price for an autographed copy they can tote on the plane with them when they leave?

Never be shy about selling your book at full retail price. You have worked hard to write and produce your book and deserve to be compensated for your efforts. The majority of the reading public will understand and appreciate this.

"There is no greater agony than bearing an untold story inside you."

—Maya Angelou

 **AUTHOR INTERVIEW**

Name: William Teie

Book Titles:
Firefighter's Handbook on Wildland Firefighting, Strategy, Tactics and Safety, Editions; First (1991), Second (2001), Third (2005), and Fourth (2018)
Leadership for a Wildland Fire Officer, Leading in a Dangerous Profession, Editions: First (2010), and Second (~2019)
History of a Place Called Rescue, (2011)

Website: deervalleypress.com

Can you tell us about your publishing journey and why you chose to self-publish your books?

In 1993, I retired after a 34-year career with the California Department of Forestry and Fire Protection. I decided to write a book on wildland firefighting, but I didn't know a thing about writing and publishing, just how to fight fire. A very close friend had written a book that was published by one of the big publishing houses. He told me about his experiences and suggested that I look into self-publishing.

I attended a two-day seminar by Dan Poynter and I was convinced that was the method I would use to produce and market the book. The book turned into 22 books over a 25-year period. I never regretted the decision to self-publish.

Self-publishing allowed me to control every aspect of the business. There is a risk in that you have to convert a lot of cash to inventory, and then have a system to store the books, take orders, accept credit cards, and fulfill and ship the orders. Yes, you will have to work harder than you would if you were just an author, but if done right, you have the ability to make more money.

I've sold well over 100,000 books. The *Firefighter's Handbook* sales have been about 47,000 copies. It's been a better experience than I ever could have expected.

What kind of business are you in and how has your book helped to grow your business?

I was retired with a good pension; my business has been mainly authoring and publishing books on firefighting. I could have used the books as a means of putting on seminars, though because I wanted to also enjoy retirement, I chose not to do that.

What have been some book marketing strategies that have generated the best results for you?

I had good name recognition in the fire service industry in the western states, so I concentrated on that by sending postcards via postal mail for the first ten years. From then on it became a word of mouth business. Since I had very little competition, once I got my foot in the door with junior colleges, I essentially had the college market to myself. And to tell the truth, I hate marketing!

Is there anything you would do differently for your next book? Any hard lessons learned?

A couple of the books took longer to sell because I didn't know the customer as well as I should have. I eventually sold the books, but it took a long time. These were not firefighting books, but books dealing with 4-wheel driving on off-road trails. I was told by Dan Poynter [publishing industry author] to keep to one field, and I violated that advice.

What advice would you offer to new authors?

If you self-publish, you MUST find an editor that will not attempt to rewrite your book in their style. Insist that they maintain your style of writing. I did have to fire an editor. Also, you need a good proofreader. Not a friend that is better with English than you are, a real proofreader. Both of these people will cost you money but having a book full of errors will kill your reputation and sales! Do it right or don't do it at all.

You have to know your potential customer. Ask yourself who would want to buy this book and why? Invest your money wisely. Don't print a thousand books that you have to pay for and store if you can't identify two-thousand potential customers. If you are not sure, print a short run of a hundred books and see how the sales go.

Understand that very few authors make a lot of money. If you self-publish you can make more. You can't ignore Amazon, but understand that they do things their way and really eat into your potential bottom line.

Try to tie your book into a speaking career. This is a perfect match, and it allows you to get out and make some more money and meet your customers.

Most important is to have FUN!

Enjoying this book?

The best way to thank a fellow author
is to post a review on Amazon!
(Pretty please? Thank you!)

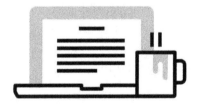

CHAPTER 10
BOOK PRINTING AND DISTRIBUTION

When it comes to deciding how you will have your book printed and distributed, the choices can be a bit overwhelming. We're going to try and simplify these for you. Essentially you have three main choices:

1. Hybrid Publisher – In this case, you would pay for a firm to produce, publish, print, and distribute your book for you. This is a great option for those who don't want to manage the details of hiring freelancers and manage the entire book production process, which as you've read in this book so far, can be overwhelming. Hiring a hybrid publisher is great for busy people who simply want it all handled in the most professional way possible.

2. POD Printing – Print on Demand (POD) print houses like IngramSpark allow you to print your books in small quantities and offer the added benefit of fulfillment to Amazon, Ingram, and other retailers. For do-it-yourself self-publishers, POD has become the leading way to produce books because of its speed, quality, and cost-efficiency.

3. Offset Printing – Before POD came along, self-publishing meant that you produced the entire book yourself and hired a printer to crank out 1,000+ copies. If you can actually sell a large number of copies quickly, can afford to print and store them, and you're willing to deal with setting up distribution to Amazon and other retailers, offset printing is still a viable option. When printing in large quantities, your per-book price will likely end up being cheaper compared to POD printing.

When printing full-color books or custom projects (like a unique trim size or specially cut covers), offset printing overseas can be cheaper. The biggest challenge with offset printing is that there is no distribution built in so once your books are printed, you have to get them distributed yourself. This can be done, but it requires that you manage inventory and form a direct relationship with wholesalers and/or Amazon and other retailers.

Let's review each of these options in greater detail.

HYBRID PUBLISHING

For nonfiction authors who are extremely busy, also running a business, or just overwhelmed by the prospect of self-publishing, hybrid publishing can be a great choice. This involves contracting with a specialty publisher to produce, print, and distribute your books for you.

You'll pay a fee up front ranging from around $5,000 to $20,000 or more. Many reputable publishers land somewhere in the middle for a package of services that can include some editing and/or proofreading, cover design, typesetting, ebook formatting, book printing, and distribution. It can also include details you don't want to hassle with like ISBN registration, barcode generation, LOC registration, indexing, ebook distribution setup, etc. In case you haven't realized it by now, publishing a book requires a lot of work!

The warning here is to avoid vanity publishing houses, and these can be tough to spot. They too will produce your book in exchange for a check, but that doesn't mean you'll get quality production or earn fair royalties on the back end. Some of these companies take advantage of authors and will publish anything in exchange for a check.

When investigating publisher options, here are some questions to ask to be sure you're getting a fair deal.

What are the terms of the contract?

Don't sign a contract that gives away your rights. If you're paying for a company to produce your book, you should retain 100% of the rights to your work. You should also have the option to cancel your contract at any time.

Unfortunately, some of these companies require authors to lock into an agreement for up to two years. That means that if Random House calls and offers you $1 million to publish your book (hey, you've got to have a dream, right?), you can't cancel your agreement and take your book elsewhere. It also means that if you're unsatisfied in any way, you're stuck with them.

How are royalties structured?

All hybrid publishers will expect to take a small percentage of the earnings from your book, and that is fair, but they shouldn't earn more than you do. Ask to see a detailed pricing breakdown and how much they will earn from your book sales. Some companies bundle a flat fee into the wholesale price of the book. Stephanie's company, Authority Publishing, earns around $1 per book sold but doesn't take any additional percentage of royalties earned. Here's an example of what this structure looks like:

Retail price:	$20
Less retailer discount of 40%:	$8
Less wholesale book print cost:	$4
Net royalty to author:	**$8**

Some publishers will take an additional percentage of the royalty. As the writer and the person paying for publishing services, you should earn more from book sales than your for-hire publisher does.

What will my books cost to purchase?
This is a very important question to ask and can help you identify if you're dealing with a vanity press. Whether your books are printed on demand or in larger quantities, a standard 150-page trade paperback with a black and white interior costs on average around $3 to $5 to print (and can cost even less if printed in quantities over 1,000). Your purchase price should be in this ballpark. If you have a black and white paperback with 200 pages or less and the publisher says that your wholesale cost is $7 or more, *turn and run the other way.*

Publishers are operating businesses, and they have every right to charge fees to keep the lights on. What they shouldn't do, however, is take advantage of inexperienced authors. If they are charging you half of your retail price, or in the neighborhood of $10 per copy for a black and white paperback book, they are taking advantage of you. Unfortunately, this is more common than it should be.

This also impacts your ability to earn a profit on your book sales. If your book is 150 pages, your retail price will likely be around $15. Remember, you have to offer retailers a discount of 40% to 55% off, which means they would pay around $7 to $9 for the book. If your print cost is $10, you can't make a profit—you'd actually lose money. As a self-published author, you should be earning a few dollars per book sold through retail channels, at a minimum, and even more for books you sell yourself.

Who sets the retail price?
You should be involved in setting the retail price for your book, and it needs to be reasonable. Using the previous example, if you publish a 150-page memoir, it should probably be priced in the $15 range. If your publisher is going to set the sale price over

$20, that's a problem. Pricing like that will prohibit buyers and cause them to question why you're charging so much.

While there are exceptions to pricing rules—for example, academic and technical books are often priced higher than other books—your retail price shouldn't be well above the standard for your genre. Check the prices for other books by your publisher and make sure they are reasonable. Note that color books and hardcovers will always be priced higher because they cost so much more to print.

Do you outsource any of your services overseas?

One way that all kinds of companies cut costs is by utilizing inexpensive labor overseas. There is nothing inherently wrong with hiring overseas workers for some tasks, but when it comes to book production, this can be a red flag.

First, there is no copyright protection for your work in other countries so if a rogue book designer is secretly reproducing your work in his country, you won't have any recourse. Also, this labor is inexpensive, sometimes they earn just a few dollars per hour. If you're spending thousands to get your book produced, you have a right to expect it to be produced by an experienced professional who is paid a fair wage.

Some publishers even outsource *editing* to non–U.S. based workers. It's completely reasonable to expect that English would be the first language of your editor. In fact, you should demand it.

How long have you been in business?

Beware of newer companies that don't have much history or financial backing. Just about anyone can start a publishing company—including you—but that doesn't mean they will still be in business in two, five or 10+ years. Many, many authors have been burned by small presses that decided to close up shop, leaving authors without their book files and payments.

Oftentimes these are shops started by an independent editor or book designer who just decided that since they were already working with authors, they might as well offer publishing services too. While not all small shops are problematic (we all start some-where), you should be really sure that your publisher is committed to the business for the long haul.

Who is your parent company?
Unfortunately, some publishing firms, including well-known and seemingly reputable companies, white-label services from bigger corporations with terrible reputations (essentially they sub-contract to other publishing firms). For example, Author Solutions, the parent company to AuthorHouse, iUniverse, Trafford Publishing, Xlibris, and others, was embroiled in a lawsuit that began in 2013 and alleged deceptive practices. By the way, Author Solutions delivers white-labeled services for Balboa Press (a division of Hay House Publishing), Archway Publishing (Simon and Schuster's self-publishing imprint), LifeRich Publishing (a division of *Reader's Digest*), and others.

In brief, the suit claimed that Author Solutions lured authors in with false claims, like saying that their books would compete with traditional publishing houses and they would earn higher royalties. It also indicated that the company's marketing services were over-promised and under-delivered. The suit was meant to be a class action brought about by several disgruntled Author Solutions clients, but a judge denied the request for class-action status.

This case was closely watched by the publishing industry, and it was eventually settled out of court in 2015. Details of the settlement were not made available.

What can you learn from this? Follow that old adage: If it sounds too good to be true, it probably is.
Also, don't let any publisher flatter you by pretending they are similar to a traditional publishing firm. At least one vanity press offers prospective authors a "symbolic book advance" of $1. Yes, a one-dollar bill. This is a sales tactic that makes authors think they've been *chosen*. Yes, chosen to open your checkbook and dole out some cash!

Before you hire any publishing service, please do two things:

- Search Google for "scam + <publisher name>," "lawsuit + <publisher name>," and "reviews + <publisher name>." You may be surprised to learn the history of some of the vanity publishing houses.

- Ask for references. Call at least a couple of authors who've published with the company. Better yet, look at book cover examples on the publisher's site and hunt down a few authors on your own—those who aren't expecting to be asked for their opinion. You might hear a horror story, or you might get a glowing review. They're not all bad, but there are definitely some shady companies out there.

The Upside of Hybrid Publishing

Don't let our warnings scare you; there are plenty of high-quality, ethical hybrid publishing firms available to help make your book a reality. Self-publishing can absolutely be overwhelming. The fact that this book you're reading now came in at over 72,000 words is evidence that there are many details that must be covered.

If you're overwhelmed by the thought of self-publishing, you're too busy, or you're just not a do-it-yourselfer, you are not alone! Don't hesitate to contract with a reputable firm to get your book done. It can potentially save you time, energy, and a lot of frustration when you have the right team of experts to carry your project to the finish line.

Shameless plug: Stephanie's firm, Authority Publishing, has offered high-quality nonfiction book production services since 2008. Visit AuthorityPublishing.com for details.

PRINT ON DEMAND PRINTING

For do-it-yourselfers, POD printing has made producing books easy and affordable. Print on demand means that you can produce books one at a time. In the early days of self-publishing, authors had to order large quantities of books—often 1,000 or more copies—delivered on pallets and stored in the garage for years.

POD has been an industry game-changer, and it eliminates major printing expenses, though books cost a little more when ordered in smaller quantities. However, the price difference is usually negligible when compared with having to shell out thousands of dollars upfront in inventory you may never sell.

Another advantage of POD is that if you decide to make changes to your book after its release, you can simply replace files with your printer and produce a new edition, without having to worry about all that inventory gathering dust in your garage. Many of the POD companies also offer direct distribution to Amazon and other online retailers, which means that you don't have to handle book distribution to those retailers yourself. When orders are placed on Amazon, the printer cranks out a copy and ships directly to the retailer, so you can just sit back and collect your payments.

There are a number of choices in POD companies, though the top three right now are IngramSpark, Lightning Source, and Kindle Direct Publishing (formerly CreateSpace), so we're going to focus on those for the purposes of this book.

Which POD firm should you choose?

Recently there has been much discussion in the publishing community around whether authors should publish their books with both IngramSpark/Lightning Source *and* Kindle Direct Publishing (KDP) or choose just one publishing platform. Below we break down some of the pros and cons you should know about.

But first, let's clarify that IngramSpark is a publishing platform for indie authors and Lightning Source, its sister company, is targeted toward more experienced publishers with multiple titles. The parent company for IngramSpark and Lightning Source is Ingram, the world's largest supplier of books to bookstores, which means that these companies offer excellent extended distribution services. When you print and distribute your titles here, your books are made available to bookstores. That doesn't mean a bookstore will necessarily carry your book, but if a reader walks into a Barnes and Noble in San Francisco, Houston, or Orlando, they can special order your book.

IngramSpark and Lightning Source compete directly with KDP, an Amazon-owned company. Working with KDP gives some competitive advantages when it comes to book sales through Amazon. However, KDP also brings some business practices that are viewed as less-than-favorable by many independent authors and publishers.

Out of Stock Issues

In recent years, Amazon has been marking some book titles—books distributed by *non*-KDP printers—as out of stock when they aren't (they can't really be out of stock when they're printed on demand). Speculation has been growing as to what is actually happening here. Some believe it's an algorithm issue with Amazon's digital stocking system that needs to be repaired. But this problem has been going on for over a year, which leads many of us to wonder if Amazon is using monopolistic practices to force indie authors to publish through KDP. Should it really take them years to correct an algorithm issue on one of the most sophisticated websites in the world?

Many of us in the publishing industry view this as an underhanded way for Amazon's KDP to force authors into publishing with them. Essentially, if you publish anywhere other than KDP, your books may show out of stock during your book launch, special promotion, or just randomly, for no apparent reason. We've seen it over and over again. This isn't a new issue, but it seems to be picking up steam. Writers Weekly addressed this issue in a 2017 blog post: writersweekly.com/ask-the-expert/unavailable-on-amazon.

One workaround some authors have adopted is to publish their books with *both* KDP and IngramSpark/Lightning Source. To do this, you would use KDP to distribute to Amazon *only* and use IngramSpark/Lightning Source to distribute everywhere else. This prevents the out of stock and shipping delay issues on Amazon while allowing you to take advantage of the excellent distribution to other retail channels available through Ingram.

It's unfortunate that Amazon is forcing some authors and publishers to take this path. If we want these business practices to change, we need to speak up. Forcing anyone to use a service is a terrible business practice.

Additional Pros and Cons

Following are some pros and cons you should know when planning to publish your books with any of these firms.

Expanded Distribution: Because IngramSpark and Lightning Source are sister organizations of Ingram, the largest supplier of books to bookstores, both offer excellent distribution to the bookstore market, libraries, and beyond. KDP offers its own "expanded distribution," but it can't match Ingram's reach. Keep in mind that traditional brick-and-mortar bookstores like Barnes and Noble don't necessarily want to do business with an Amazon-owned company (KDP). Having this imprint on your book can actually hurt your ability to get distribution.

Retailer Discounts: You can set your own retailer discount with Lightning Source and IngramSpark, which is important if you plan to distribute your books to the retail market. Most brick-and-mortar bookstores require at least a 40% discount off the retail price, which you cannot set with KDP. In fact, KDP only offers retailers 25% off, which most brick-and-mortar stores won't touch, further limiting your ability to have bookstores carry KDP books.

In addition, Amazon wants authors and publishers to give them 55% off retail, but you don't necessarily have to comply with this. Karl and Stephanie have both always set our retail discounts at 40% through Lightning Source, and Amazon still lists our books and even discounts them.

Setting your retail discount with Lightning Source and IngramSpark at a minimum of 30% will make your book available to Amazon and other retailers, though it won't guarantee they will list the title. Setting your discount at 53% will ensure that a 40% discount passes through to retailers, after Ingram takes its piece of the pie. If brick-and-mortar retailers are a target for you, set your discount at 53%, but if you're focusing on online sales, you can set it lower. Ultimately your discount is up to you, but we recommend somewhere between 40% and 55%.

Book Royalties: Depending on how you set your retailer discount, you can potentially earn more book royalties when publishing through Lightning Source and IngramSpark. KDP takes 40% of the retail price when your books are sold directly to Amazon customers, but it takes 60% when your books are sold through expanded distribution. With Lightning Source and IngramSpark, you can set your discount at any percent you choose (which can help boost sales with non-Amazon retailers). You should do the math on your own book first to determine which channel will be more profitable for you.

Royalties from Retail Distribution: KDP significantly lowers the amount of profit earned by authors when sold via distribution to other retailers, while Lightning Source and IngramSpark authors earn higher royalty payments. If you sell a significant number of books to non-Amazon retailers, the difference in earnings can be substantial.

Returnable Books and Retailers: You can choose to accept returns on Lightning Source and IngramSpark titles, which makes your book more attractive to retailers. We discuss returns in greater detail in Chapter 11, but you should know that no brick-and-mortar bookstore wants to order non-returnable books. So, if bookstores are a primary target for you, Lightning Source and IngramSpark bring a big advantage.

Amazon Pre-Sales: Both Lightning Source and IngramSpark allow authors/publishers to set up pre-sales on Amazon weeks or even months in advance of your book's official release date. Note that you have to have your book files print-ready in order to do this.

When you set up a pre-sale, you can set a release date in the future and begin pre-promotion efforts. Generating pre-sales, which allow buyers to commit to purchase the book when it officially goes on sale, means that all of those preorders are billed on the day your book is officially released—and all those sales on release day count toward your ranking on Amazon bestseller lists. This can be advantageous if you have a solid pre-sale marketing campaign.

Oddly enough, KDP does *not* currently offer pre-sales, however you can set up a pre-sale for the Kindle edition of your book.

Hardcover Printing: Both Lightning Source and IngramSpark offer hardcover printing, while KDP does not.

Bulk Printing Discounts: KDP pricing is not competitive compared to the high-volume print discounts offered by Lightning Source and IngramSpark, so if you plan to order your books in quantities of 500+, pricing will likely be better with Lightning Source and IngramSpark.

Color Printing: If your book interior is printed in color, you'll get far better printing prices from Lightning Source and IngramSpark, as much as 50% less than KDP. Lightning Source and IngramSpark also offer low-cost and premium color printing options.

Setup Fees: Lightning Source and IngramSpark both charge setup fees of around $49 for new titles, while KDP doesn't charge a fee. However, IngramSpark refunds the setup fee when an order for 50 copies is placed within 60 days of setup, so essentially this is free as well. And when you compare royalties earned, those fees can often be earned back quickly when book sales are generated. (Also note that members of the Nonfiction Authors Association get free title setup with IngramSpark.)

Reputation: KDP has a long-standing reputation problem within the publishing industry. Barnes and Noble and many indie booksellers don't want to stock KDP titles, which makes sense. Why would they support a division of their largest competitor? A quick Google search will show you many articles and blog posts about KDP books being rejected by bookstores of all sizes.

ISBNs: KDP offers free ISBNs, while Lightning Source and IngramSpark do not. However, one important tip, no matter which publishing service you use, is that _you should ALWAYS acquire your own ISBN_. ISBNs are linked to the publisher where they originated, so you should absolutely avoid using one issued by KDP or any other free source since that associates your book with that publisher for all eternity. Instead, purchase your own block of ISBNs and establish your own publishing company name—something that sounds like a legitimate publishing firm. U.S. authors can purchase ISBNs from Bowkers: MyIdentifiers.com and Canadian authors can purchase ISBNs here: bac-lac.gc.ca.

Printing: Oddly enough, KDP contracts some of its book printing to Ingram. It's an unusual relationship, to say the least.

Drop Shipping and Overseas Printing: One more advantage that IngramSpark and Lightning Source offer is the ability to drop-ship books to any location quickly (within a few business days). They also have print facilities in England, France, and Australia so you can save on shipping costs to these countries if you sell books or conduct events there.

As fellow authors and publishers, our opinion is that IngramSpark and Lightning Source are much better choices for publishing versus KDP, largely due to the unfair practices Amazon is using to give KDP books an advantage on the site, but also because IngramSpark/Lightning Source offer higher quality printing, better options for trim sizes, hardcover and color printing, and deliver excellent expanded distribution services.

At this time, due to the out of stock issues on Amazon, we are currently recommending that authors publish with both IngramSpark and KDP. Again, take advantage of the expanded distribution IngramSpark offers. With KDP, choose their Amazon distribution only, not their so-called "expanded" distribution.

These issues are evolving and changing. For the latest news on publishing options, follow the blog at NonfictionAuthorsAssociation.com.

Lightning Source, IngramSpark and KDP aren't the only POD printers, but they are currently the largest players in this space. Do your homework if you want to consider other options.

OFFSET PRINTING

There are hundreds, if not thousands, of book printers across the U.S. and in other countries. Before print on demand came along, self-published authors would find a local printer to produce their books. You can still do this today, though in many cases, you'll need to order larger quantities of books at a time—often 1,000 copies or more.

Benefits of Offset Printing

- **Better per-book pricing.** When you print anything in larger quantities, be it flyers, t-shirts or books, the price goes down. If you plan to handle your own book distribution and you have the budget and space available to store large quantities of books, offset printing may make sense for you.

- **More custom options.** Maybe you want an unusual trim size for your book or you want your cover to have a custom cut-out feature. POD printing is limited to a small number of standard print sizes and only a few printing options for covers, while offset printing can offer all kinds of specialty choices from pop-up inserts in books to leather or velvet trim on covers.

- **Lower cost color printing.** If you're producing cookbooks, children's books, coffee-table books or other books that require full-color interiors and a large number of pages, you should definitely investigate offset printing. Full-color printing usually costs more than twice what black and white printing costs, especially in POD, and you can potentially save $10 or more per book by printing in large quantities with an offset printer. This is also an area where many self-publishers end up having their books printed overseas because color printing there can be significantly cheaper, even after you factor in shipping fees and the time it takes to get through customs. For color books, do your homework and get several quotes. Also, talk to other authors and get recommendations for printing services.

Downside of Offset Printing

- **Bigger up-front expense.** Because you'll be required to order 1,000, 3,000 or even 5,000 copies at once, you'll need to have the cash to purchase the books.

- **Requires storage.** You'll either need to take over your garage with pallets of books or locate climate-controlled warehouse space to store them. (The garage is actually a terrible option since climate can age books quickly.)

- **Increased risk.** Having thousands of books in storage means that your inventory is at risk of natural disaster, damage from elements (extreme heat, cold temps, or moisture), and aging. Plenty of authors have had books stored in their garages for 10+ years, and that means the interior pages have likely yellowed, the covers have faded, and they may even have developed a musty odor.

- **Changes become costly.** If you ever want to revise your book, correct errors, or update information, you'll be faced with the issue of liquidating or destroying your inventory.

- **Shipping and distribution.** When you are your own publisher and distributor, you have to deal with shipping books to retailers, individual buyers, etc. Ask yourself if this is a job you really want to handle. For some who have the time or a staff to help, this isn't an issue. But it's a challenge for most of us.

We maintain a list of over 200 book printers around the world. If you'd like to investigate your options, download a free copy here: nonfictionauthorsassociation.com/reader-bonus.

Ultimately, only you can decide whether hybrid publishing, POD printing, or offset printing is best for you. Hopefully you now have a better understanding of your options so you can make an informed decision that won't leave you with regrets down the road.

PHYSICAL PROOFS

Before you approve your digital book files for final printing and distribution, it's essential that you order a physical "proof" of the book, which is simply a single printed copy. You'll want to be sure the book prints properly and that bleed/trim looks good, pages are uniform, and that there are no glaring errors you missed when reviewing the digital files.

When possible, plan some extra time in your publishing timeline to allow for revisions at this stage. Ideally, your proof will print perfectly and no changes will be needed, but in reality, you may need to make some adjustments.

ADVANCED READER COPIES (ARCS)

Advanced Reader Copies, known in the publishing industry as ARCs, are typically used for publicity purposes. If you're seeking book reviews upon the release of your book, or if you're working with a publicist on generating media opportunities, you'll need to print some ARCs.

ARCs are usually printed several months before the book is released, which gives publicists and media outlets time to plan for the book release. Advanced copies don't have to be fully edited or even have a finished cover design. In fact, media pros expect ARCs to be in various stages of development. The good news is that the world of digital printing allows you to print copies of your book at any stage in the process.

When producing ARCs, be sure to note on the cover and in the opening page: "Advanced Reader Copy – Not for Resale." You don't want unedited or incomplete copies of your book getting circulated for sale in the used book market.

Of course, you may want to skip printing ARCs if you don't have a need for them. They are entirely optional.

 PRO TIP: *Manage file delivery.*

Avoid sending out Word documents or text documents to your reviewers and instead send PDFs that can't be edited. This is a minor point, but you don't want anyone to be able to make changes to your document and pass it on, potentially misrepresenting your work. Again, this is a minor concern, but a good practice. PDFs also allow a file to be viewed correctly on any device, whether a PC, Mac, tablet, or phone.

"Happiness lies in the joy of achievement and the thrill of creative effort."

—Franklin D. Roosevelt

CHAPTER 11
BOOKSTORE DISTRIBUTION AND BEYOND

Whether or not brick-and-mortar bookstore distribution is a goal for you, it's important to understand how distribution works. Bookstores aren't the only place to sell books, and they're often not even the best place to sell them.

Let's go back to the beginning:

- Why did you write your book?

- What's your ultimate goal for your book?

- Is it part of your life's vision and passion?

- Do you want to use it as a calling card for your business?

- Do you want to break into a new business?

- Do you want to position yourself as an expert in your field?

- Do you want to create new income streams?

No matter what you answer, you're going to find yourself distributing your book through several channels. The percentage of books distributed through each channel will vary depending on the business you're in and your answer to the questions above.

Here are the primary ways you will distribute your book:

- Amazon
- Other online bookstores (BN.com, etc.)
- Trunk of your car (seriously!)
- Back of the room (after speaking)
- From your website
- From other websites
- Direct from the printer (if print on demand)
- Smashwords and other ebook sites

Other possible options:

- Brick-and-mortar bookstores
- Brick-and-mortar retailers including gift shops, grocery stores, chain stores, hospital gift shops, restaurants, gas stations, beauty salons, auto parts stores, drugstores, donut shops, bike shops, airport bookstores, big-box stores, etc.
- Trade associations
- Nonprofits
- Historical societies
- Military retailers
- Museums
- Libraries
- Trade shows, festivals, and related events

- Schools and colleges

- Specialty sales market (promotional products)

For example, Karl sells some technology books by other authors and publishers through his website. His arrangement is very simple: he buys their books at a standard 40% discount and sells them at whatever price he chooses. If their books never sell, he's stuck with them. So, for these authors, he serves as a distribution channel.

The most profitable option will always be to sell books directly to buyers at speaking engagements or from your own website. When you sell directly, you don't have to share any percentage of the sale, thus guaranteeing you get paid full price. Authors will always make more money when selling books directly to buyers.

SHOULD I SEEK BOOKSTORE DISTRIBUTION FOR MY BOOK?

Many self-published authors want to know how to get bookstores to carry their books. The traditional way to do this is to work with a book distributor. These companies employ salespeople who go out and convince bookstore buyers—and other types of retailers—to carry new books.

Distributors can have a specialty focus area, such as children's books, cookbooks, travel guides or health books. They can also serve a variety of markets such as colleges, gift shops, specialty retail, the military market, and so on.

Working with a distributor to get placement in bookstores and other retail outlets is not impossible, but there are some pros and cons to consider.

THE UPSIDE OF BOOK DISTRIBUTORS

- Potentially reach more readers.

- Potentially sell more copies and earn more money.

- Be able to tell people your book is available in stores.

THE DOWNSIDE OF BOOK DISTRIBUTORS

- Distributors take *65% to 75% off the retail price*. Remember, they have to offer retailers 40% to 55% off retail price and the distributor needs to earn a piece of the action, too. This means you have to leave plenty of room in your retail pricing for profit.

- Just like agents and publishers, distributors will require proof of marketing and publicity activities in order to get accepted into their program.

- You will typically need to print 1,000 or more copies to be warehoused while the distributor's sales force goes out looking for buyers (plan for a significant investment on your part).

- Just because a book is available in a bookstore, it doesn't mean that it will sell. With so much competition on the shelves, you still have to create demand so that buyers go out looking for your book.

- If a bookstore decides to carry your book and it doesn't sell well within a few months, all copies will get returned and you will have to issue a full refund. Worse, books are typically shipped back haphazardly so they're often damaged and unsellable.

  Unfortunately, books are one of the few items in all of retail where stores expect to receive a full refund if inventory doesn't move. The clothing industry doesn't do this. When Macy's decides it's done selling a line of jeans, for example, it's resold to a discount buyer, such as T.J. Maxx or Marshalls. But when Barnes and Noble decides a book isn't selling fast enough, it tosses remaining copies into boxes to ship back to the publisher or distributor.

Book distributors are selective about the titles they carry, so you will have to convince them to consider yours. You'll need to show your marketing and publicity plans, and demonstrate you have a platform. They don't want to place books that are going to get returned so they need some assurance that the author is helping to generate sales demand.

There are exceptions to this rule, though. If you've heeded our advice and have chosen a well-defined niche, you may have luck getting distributors who specialize in gift shops, hospitals, hardware stores, or other non-bookstore markets. Niche titles can have all kinds of sale advantages, especially if there isn't a lot of competition for your title, and even if you lack a coveted author "platform."

For example, if you publish books about gardening in California, you may find a distributor with relationships with California hardware stores, nurseries, and gift shops—and they may be thrilled to place your book because they already have many connections in this category. The same is true for all kinds of niche books. Here are some examples:

- Cookbooks covering food allergies.

- Pet-care books focused on specific breeds or exotic animals.

- Books about specific kinds of crafts or hobbies.

- Health guides focused on specific conditions like Cushing's disease or gastritis.

- A memoir about owning a bed and breakfast.

- Technology books covering specific software tools.

- Local travel or history books.

These are just a sampling of the types of niche books that could potentially find a home with a distributor. If you've got a niche title, it will quite likely increase your chances of locating a distribution partner.

For a list of the top distributors specializing in bookstores, gift shops, the college market, and more, download our free guide here: nonfictionauthorsassociation.com/reader-bonus.

AN ALTERNATIVE TO CONSIDER: *Reverse Bookstore Demand*

Because it's not easy to form a relationship with book distributors, and they also get such a large cut of the revenue, another option is to create *reverse* bookstore demand. When lots of people request your book at Barnes and Noble, the store will eventually contact you about carrying your book and will usually be willing to buy from you directly, at least initially.

If the store believes your book has long-term sales potential, they will likely connect you with one of their preferred distributors and recommend that you set up an alliance with them (an automatic "in" with the distributor, but again, you have to increase your discount since they need to earn a cut too).

In the best-case scenario, you'd form an agreement directly with the retailer, offering them 40% to 50% off the retail price (industry standard rate). Keep in mind that traditional bookstores will also require the option to return books, and you will have no choice but to agree to do so and then cross your fingers and hope your books sell like popcorn at a Star Wars premiere.

Reverse demand can work if you're building your platform, getting media coverage, and generating demand for your book in stores. This isn't a myth—we've heard success stories from authors many times.

For a fascinating case study on reverse bookstore demand, read our interview with author Mike Michalowicz at the end of this chapter.

WHAT HAPPENS IF YOU IGNORE BOOKSTORES?

While you may have a dream of seeing your book on store shelves, and from experience we can tell you that it is indeed a great feeling, it may not be the best use of your time and effort. According to AuthorEarnings.com, a full 45% of all print book sales in 2017 came from Amazon. Take that in for a moment. Nearly half of ALL paperbacks and hardcovers are purchased online through Amazon.

The remaining 55% of print book sales are divided up between small and large brick anned mortar bookstores, warehouse stores like Costco, other retailers like Target and Walmart, plus schools, colleges, and other non-bookstore outlets.

Bottom line: Nobody has a larger share of the book market than Amazon.

Diving deeper into the online book sales market, ebooks accounted for 55% of online book sales, audiobooks accounted for 6%, and print books accounted for the remaining 39% of units. It's also interesting to note that AuthorEarnings.com tabulated total ebook sales by publisher type and the results are fascinating. The big five publishers combined (Hachette, HarperCollins, Macmillan, Penguin Random House, and Simon and Schuster) accounted for 25.6% of all ebook sales in 2017.

But here's some exciting news: independent authors, either with a self-publishing imprint or no publisher listed, generated *a combined total of 35.9% of all ebook sales.* That's more indie author book sales than The Big Five combined! Amazon Publishing (Kindle Direct Publishing) earned 9.8% of all book sales, and the fact is that the majority of those sales came from indie authors, too.

When you factor all these sales figures together, the writing is on the wall, and it has been for a while. Sadly (for those of us who still love to stroll through a store), bookstores aren't where most people are buying books. So, the question is this: why focus your efforts there when you could put your energy into online promotion and sales?

Most books in general aren't bought on a whim. Sure, people browsing in a bookstore may pick up a few unplanned titles periodically, but for the most part, we buy books based on recommendation or a need. Recommendations can come in the form of word-of-mouth, a book review, suggestion by a trusted blogger, or directly from an author whom the reader follows and admires.

Do you really need bookstore placement? For most indie authors, the answer is probably not.

DISTRIBUTE DIRECTLY TO AMAZON

If you print books with an offset printer and don't have the advantage of POD distribution directly to Amazon, then you will have to set up direct distribution to Amazon yourself. To do this, you will need to sign up with the Amazon Advantage program: advantage.amazon.com.

With the Advantage program, you will place your books on consignment with Amazon at a 55% discount off the retail price and also pay an annual program fee of $99. Amazon will order a couple of copies to start, and you will pay to ship those to their fulfillment house. When copies sell out, they will order more, and you will again have to pay to ship them to Amazon—usually in small quantities of just a few copies.

If you begin to consistently generate a higher volume of sales, the hope is that Amazon will order larger quantities of books from you each time. However, authors who use the Advantage program have reported frustrations with how Amazon requests new book shipments—sometimes twice weekly—rather than placing an order for a month's worth of books and saving shipping costs for the author/publisher. Keep your expectations low when it comes to dealing with Amazon.

You could consider participating in the Fulfillment by Amazon program, where you ship larger quantities of your books to Amazon's warehouse and let them fulfill orders; however, their fees for this service can be prohibitive. They currently charge $2.41 per item under one pound, plus charge a monthly warehousing fee of $.69 per cubic foot.

The bottom line is if you want your books sold on Amazon, and you don't have a POD company or distributor to handle it for you, you'll have to participate in the Advantage program.

TIPS FOR DISTRIBUTION SUCCESS

Make sure your self-published book is professionally produced, from editing to typesetting to cover. Though the stigma of self-publishing has improved greatly over the years, stores (and distributors) won't touch titles that have errors or are obviously self-published.

Also, your publishing company imprint matters. Many distributors and bookstores won't consider books produced by some of the "big box" self-publishing firms (like KDP).

As with nearly everything in publishing, a lot of the success you'll have comes down to your platform. You need to be building an audience and generating demand, whether through a high-traffic website, a popular column you write for a major publication, a large presence on social media or YouTube, lots of media interviews, etc. It's important that you generate buyers for your books—and that they walk into bookstores and *ask* for your book.

"If there's a book you want to read, but it hasn't been written yet, then you must write it."

—Toni Morrison

 # AUTHOR INTERVIEW

Name: Mike Michalowicz

Book titles:
Clockwork: Design Your Business to Run Itself
Profit First: Transform Your Business from a Cash-Eating Monster to a Money-Making Machine
The Pumpkin Plan: A Simple Strategy to Grow a Remarkable Business in Any Field

Website: mikemichalowicz.com

Can you tell us about your publishing journey and why you chose to self-publish your book?

When I wrote my very first book, *The Toilet Paper Entrepreneur,* my intention was to get a mainstream publisher. I wanted to be a significant author, meaning I wanted to be one of the big authorities in the small business space. So, I wrote *The Toilet Paper Entrepreneur*, and then did everything backwards.

I thought you first wrote a book and then you find a publisher, so I wrote the book and I went to the publishers and basically got laughed out of the room because I didn't have a following or a constituency. The big question was "How big is your *platform?*" They wanted to know how many people will buy books at a guaranteed level. And since I didn't have that, I was forced into self-publishing.

With self-publishing, there are strategic advantages. You can write stylistically how you want it. And the big thing for *The Toilet Paper Entrepreneur* is I wanted a kind of contrarian book, a book that was just different than the standard fare. Many books in the business space are cerebral; almost like they've been written by professors. I wanted to write a book that was kind of street-level entrepreneurship. Self-publishing allowed me to do my book in the way I wanted.

With self-publishing you can move much more rapidly, too. I work with a major publisher now, Penguin Random House, and a book's cycle is about a year and a half from concept to actually getting it into the bookstores. With a self-published book, you can get it done in six months, even three months. You still have to invest the time in writing a high-quality book, that doesn't change, but all of the red tape, all of the queues you get stuck in, they go away, and you can move much more rapidly and dynamically.

So, self-publishing has those advantages, and I'm a big fan of self-publishing. I self-published three books and have three books that are traditionally published. Now that my platform is at its size, I anticipate that I'll be publishing through a traditional publisher through the entirety of my career, because there are advantages as you get a bigger platform.

The biggest advantage with a traditional publisher is international distribution. I can do it through self-publishing too by the way, and I have, but it's easier with the traditional route. They have all the systems in place to manage the distribution, which is important when you're selling a lot of books.

What kind of business are you in? And how have your books helped you grow your business?

I am an author, and that's a funny question because a lot of people say I am an entrepreneur who's written a book. My primary business is writing books and, knock on wood, I've made an income that is sustainable just through books. If I did nothing else, and the only thing I did was write and sell books, I could live off of it comfortably.

The flip side, or the benefit of course, is speaking. So, as I gain more notoriety, I get invited to the higher-profile, higher-paid speaking events. In fact, I'm just back from EntreLeadership, an event hosted by Dave Ramsey, who's very famous in the personal finance space. He is one of the top authorities, if not *the* authority. And at that conference of course Dave Ramsey spoke, Seth Godin spoke, Condoleezza Rice spoke, other superstars from the corporate world spoke, and I spoke. I had an opportunity to play at that level of platform because of my books.

I'm just starting to break into that category now. I even got an endorsement for my newest book from Simon Sinek, who is a category-leading author for the small business space. So, the kind of business I'm in is the business of selling books, and my books help sell more books. I have five active books, one I self-published—and that one got acquired by a traditional publisher so I did a revised, expanded edition.

What's coming out of all of this, too, is that I now have licensing deals. This means that businesses have acquired the rights to teach my books, and I do exclusive licensing deals with them. For my new book *Clockwork*, there's an individual who has licensed the content and is going to represent it on a national and international basis. There's also a company that acquired the rights to *The Pumpkin Plan* doing the same thing. *Profit First,* my most successful book to date, is handled by a company called Profit First Professionals, which in this case is not just a licensing arrangement; I am an owner in that business.

My experience is that books help sell books, but books also bring exposure. I don't focus on bulk sales, except during the launch of a new book. I primarily focus on acceptance in the small business market. I want to build a compendium of books for them, so the more books I write that serve the small business market, the more they become aware of me, and then they discover the previous books, and the books sell more books.

What have been some book marketing strategies that have generated the best results for you?

This is my favorite category. First of all is my own website. Websites are very important, and the consistency of the brand is absolutely critical. So, my website is one of the most unique business author websites out there. It's authentic and true to who I am, but it's also different than all the alternatives out there, so it becomes recognized, it becomes noticed.

The other book marketing strategy, and this is kind of book marketing 101, but it's powerful, is to associate with other peers. Get other authors to promote and support you as you promote and support them. We as authors are in what I believe to be the most unique industry, in that we really don't have competition. In my old business, I was a computer network integrator, meaning I was a computer guy. When I had a competitor who also did network integration, either he got the work or I got the work. So, I would try to beat him.

What happens as an author is when another author in my space sells their book, if their book is a good book, it engages the reader and they start seeking out more knowledge in that space, and they look for more good books. So, the funny thing is if my "competitors" or other authors in my space are doing well, by default I'll do well.

Not all authors get this, but what we need to do for marketing is find other authors and collaborate with them. They promote your book launch and you promote theirs, and I know this from experience. Every time I promote someone's book launch, I get more book sales, so it's a win-win. It's the coolest space because it's highly collaborative. Not all authors get it, and the ones who don't, I ultimately just don't work with.

But most authors do get it, and the ones who do are great. But the other thing I found is there are different tiers of authors. When I was starting out, I couldn't go to someone who had an established book out and ask them to promote because I was just a brand-new startup. So, you have to kind of scratch your way in.

I can't go to Malcolm Gladwell and say, "Hey, would you promote my book?" But I intend to be performing at that level. What I do is I circulate with authors who are performing at a similar level, meaning they have the same amount of book distribution and awareness about themselves, plus some. Someone who is a couple steps ahead of me but still willing to support me and I of course will support them. That's what has helped me step my way up in marketing.

The other thing I've done is use guerilla tactics. Here's one I've done, and I don't need to do it anymore, but it worked extremely well. I took my first self-published book to Barnes and Noble by calling and asking if they would be so kind as to promote my book by stocking it on their shelves. They literally laughed me off the phone call (with their small business division). They said they don't take self-published books, and they definitely don't take books from authors who are not established, so good luck (paraphrasing here!).

And so, I had copies of my self-published books in my garage, basement, bedroom, and kitchen—they were all packed with books. So, with the help of some friends, I went to about forty Barnes and Noble stores in our area, and we snuck books *into* the store. Not just one book, but like a fifteen pack, and started stocking the shelves.

I'll never forget the story. Someone went to the store here in Morris Plains, New Jersey, saw ten copies of my books on the shelf, and tried to buy one. When he went to pay for it, the cashier rang it up and said, "Sorry, we don't sell this." The customer pointed out the book was shelved in the store.

The clerk replied, "I realize that, but we don't sell it."

There was total confusion and the manager came out to address the customer. Can you imagine? The whole Barnes and Noble staff is now focusing on my book. And I heard from several customers that similar scenes happened in other stores.

Well, fast-forward about three months after doing this. My friends and I keep on going and restocking books at various stores. And by the way, I don't know if it's illegal to stock shelves like this. It's not like I was stealing, I was doing the reverse, misappropriation of shelving space or something. Anyway, eventually the Barnes and Noble small business division called.

I remember the phone ringing and the caller ID pops up and my hand is shaking because it's them. The first words out of her mouth were, "Hi, we have a problem." And I'm thinking, *oh my gosh, I'm about to get sued*. "We seem to be selling your book, but it's not properly inventoried with us, and we're depleted on inventory. We need three thousand copies immediately."

This was right before the Christmas rush. I was blown away, so I said, "Okay, how do I do it?" And she said, "Just have the distributor re-sync up your account with us." I had to confess that I didn't have a distributor.

"What? How did your books get into our stores? There must be an error on our side. We will take care of this and get you a distributor lined up, we'll take care of everything."

And sure enough, they got me a distributor. Within two days there was an 18-wheeler pulling up to my house to pick up two pallets of 3,000-plus books. And they continued to replenish inventory over time.

That book, *The Toilet Paper Entrepreneur,* was put front and center at the Barnes and Noble stores alongside another book by Gary Vaynerchuk called *Crush It.* It was crazy to go into the store and see *Toilet Paper Entrepreneur* right next to his. It was massive, and that was one thing that spring-boarded the popularity of *The Toilet Paper Entrepreneur.* That's the guerilla stuff that I love to do.

Is there anything you would do differently for your next book? Or any hard lessons learned?

Profit First has been my most successful book. It's sold well over 50,000 print copies in the first year. And the Audible version is probably another 80,000 copies. So, it's around 130,000 books just in English. And it's been translated into about 15 languages already.

But the big learning lesson came from my prior book, *Surge.* With that book, I did two things wrong. First of all, I got cocky. *Pumpkin Plan* was doing well and *Toilet Paper Entrepreneur* was doing well. I self-published *Profit First* and it was doing well, and then I followed it with *Surge.*

When I wrote *Surge,* I'd just had momentum with *Profit First* and all the different things I was doing, so I thought, *Ah, this book is just going to crush it. I'm just going to launch it.* I didn't make any effort to build a marketing campaign. I didn't build the rapport with authors or ask anyone to help promote it. I just put the book out there and it fizzled.

The second problem was that it's not a good book. It's a good book in theory—meaning the way it presents itself. But it's not a good book in that it's not consistent with my brand. All my other books are very actionable. They talk about how to do step-by-step processes. I simplify things for readers.

Surge is a much more theoretical book, and this is not who I am as an author, so there's an inconsistency. So, it's not resonating with people and that's why *Surge* is a failure.

Now I use it in other ways. I share the book for free and I use it as a marketing piece. It still sells on Amazon, but you know, it's about one print book every five days. It's basically dead. I put a lot of money into *Surge.* As a self-published author, you've got to print the books, you've got to put in a lot of time writing the books, so that was a hard-learned lesson.

I'm now working on my newest book *Clockwork.* I've put almost a year of marketing planning into it already and I've still got three months before the launch.

What advice would you offer to new authors?

I think you can choose to be an author or a writer, and I believe they're different. I think people author books, and I think countless people write books. I think an author is a person who devotes their career to the creation of books, but also to the marketing and promotion involved in circulating that idea. Authorship to me is not just writing a book; authorship is a lifestyle. It's an all-in commitment.

I've always wanted to be an author, and ten years ago I made the commitment to do so. I decided to go all-in on this. My full-time career is being an author, and I see my books as something that will live on beyond my life, something that will continue to impact lives. And I make every effort, every day, to support and promote the concepts further.

My suggestion to new authors is make a decision. Do you want to be a writer? That's fine if you want to write a book and have it out there for purposes of just writing a book, or whatever purpose it serves. Or, do you want to be an author and devote your career to it? If you choose to devote your career to being an author, and realize you're not just writing books, you're marketing concepts, you've got to be circulating those concepts and getting the word out in a big way.

CHAPTER 12
EBOOKS AND AUDIOBOOKS

There's good news and bad news with regard to electronic books. The good news is that you have many, many options for distributing your works. And each of those is an opportunity to build your personal brand and make money. The bad news is that there are more than a dozen formats that your book can be distributed in. You need to decide whether it's worth your time and trouble to publish in all these formats.

The biggest ebook readers right now are the Kindle (by Amazon), the Nook (by Barnes and Noble), the iPad (by Apple), and good old PDF format. As with everything else, there's a learning curve to creating your book in all these formats.

UNDERSTANDING EBOOK FILE FORMATS

Ebook file format types include Mobi/ADW, Epub, Word documents, PDF, and some proprietary formats required by specific vendors. Since the technology changes constantly, and we aren't super fans of do-it-yourself book production, we are not including instructions for how to format files. You can easily Google instructions and attempt to do it yourself, though we recommend hiring an experienced ebook formatter to handle this for you. Your book typesetter will likely be experienced at ebook formatting and will handle that for you as part of their standard service package.

With that said, you should understand your options and how ebook distribution works. Here are the top ebook vendors and the formats they require:

Amazon Kindle Direct Publishing: KDP.Amazon.com

Formats Accepted: Mobi/ADW

Royalties: If your book is priced between $2.99 and $9.99, you will receive 70% of U.S. sales minus a small file delivery fee. For all other Kindle pricing, 35% royalty rate.

Barnes and Noble Nook: press.barnesandnoble.com

Epub 2 and Word documents

Royalties: If your book is priced between $2.99 and $9.99, you will receive 65%. For all other pricing, 40% royalty rate.

Apple iBookstore: itunes.com/sellyourbooks

Epub 2 and 3, iBooks Author

Royalties: 70%

Rakuten Kobo Store: kobo.com/us/en/p/writinglife

Epub 2 and 3, and Word documents

Royalties: If your book is priced between $2.99 and $12.99, you will receive 65%. For all other pricing, 45% royalty rate.

Google Play: play.google.com/books/publish/

Epub 2 and 3

Royalties: 52%

EBOOK DISTRIBUTION PARTNER

One of the most popular services for putting your ebook into all the top ebook formats is Smashwords (smashwords.com). Smashwords allows you to import a single Word file, formatted to their standards, and its proprietary system manually converts that file into a variety of formats. Then, Smashwords distributes your ebooks to all the major ebook retailers, *except* Amazon. Smashwords is easy to use, free to get started, and pays royalties at 85% of the net they receive from each vendor.

If you want to avoid formatting and distributing ebooks to multiple vendors, you can cover your bases by a combination of publishing directly to Kindle and Smashwords. This is what we do and what we most often recommend.

Another option is Draft2Digital (draft2digital.com), which works much like Smashwords, except that they keep about 10% of your retail price. Book Baby (bookbaby.com) is another ebook distributor. They charge an up-front fee for ebook formatting and distribution, around $250 for a 200-page book, but don't charge any royalties on sales.

THE LIBRARY MARKET

Libraries purchase ebooks and lend them out, one ebook at a time, just as they do with print books. There are several vendors that manage ebook sales to libraries. If this is a target market for you, consider contacting them to find out their current requirements for distribution.

Rakuten OverDrive – Overdrive.com
Note that Smashwords and Draft2Digital both distribute ebooks to OverDrive.

ProQuest – proquest.com/about/publishers-partners
Distributes ebooks to over 26,000 libraries, university libraries, and other research organizations.

Bibliotheca – bibliotheca.com
Distributes to over 500 libraries.

DIGITAL RIGHTS MANAGEMENT (DRM)

Digital Rights Management (DRM) refers to the protection of intellectual property by electronic means. For example, if you buy a book through Amazon's Kindle program, you can read it on your phone or on your Kindle. You cannot legally make a copy in PDF format and give a copy to each of your friends.

You might be *able* to crack some codes and distribute the files, but that doesn't make it legal or ethical. DRM attempts to limit the ways in which electronic products are distributed.

The reason that DRM exists is that it is so easy to make illegal copies of books (and other electronic products) today. A small group of people make the intellectual argument that they have a right to everyone else's works without paying for them. But mostly the people violating copyright simply don't understand that they are depriving the author of money.

We've seen this with software and music downloads already. Remember Napster, the free music download service that allowed users to share their song files online? In 2001, a judge ruled that Napster infringed on the copyrights of song owners. It was a landmark intellectual property case that raised awareness about the dangers of sharing content, like music and ebooks, without permission from the copyright owner.

As an author, you probably want to protect your work from free distribution. Know that the big publishing houses like Amazon, Apple, and so forth are developing and implementing standards that protect you as much as they protect themselves. Our feeling is that DRM is a lot less of an issue in the nonfiction world than in the world of fiction.

One of Karl's books was originally a series of blog posts. He gathered up all those blog posts, put them into logical order, and reposted them on his website. Then he turned them into a book in PDF format (for sale). He followed that by creating the printed book version, an audiobook on CD, an audio download, and ebook versions for Kindle and Smashwords. Since his target audience consists of professional computer technicians, if someone wanted to turn his book into a widely available PDF download, it would be extremely easy to do.

As a result, you can get this book in the following formats:

- Free as a web page download

- Free as a series of blog posts

- Book for $19.95

- Audiobook for $19.95

- Ebook (PDF) for $19.95

- Amazon Kindle for $19.95

- Smashwords (many formats) for $19.95

On several occasions, Karl has also offered the book free as part of a promotion with some large partners. So, it's sometimes used to simply build his mailing list.

The result? This book sells like crazy! The price is reasonable. Almost everyone who buys the audiobook also buys the PDF or physical book. So, the average buyer actually purchases the book more than once, even though it's no secret that it's *available for free on his blog*. This has been going on for more than ten years.

After the initial release and six months of spectacular sales, Karl now sells about three of these books nearly every single day, 365 days a year. He's not getting rich on this. His profit after shipping, printing, marketing, and generally managing this book is under $10 per copy. But it keeps him in lattes!

During the 2017 Nonfiction Writers Conference, keynote speaker Seth Godin gave us all a memorable quote: ***Your problem is not piracy. Your problem is obscurity.*** He went on to suggest that authors should give their books away for free as much as possible, because the more people who read your book, the better your chances of building word of mouth.

We believe in this concept so much that we WANT you to share this book with a friend. If you have it in PDF, email it to every author you know.

The lesson: Free distribution is not going to kill your sales. You may want to make some effort at digital rights management, but don't lose sleep over it. We don't.

EBOOK PRICING

Amazon has played a big part in driving down the cost of ebooks. It rewards authors and publishers when we price Kindle books between $2.99 and $9.99 by giving us a royalty rate of 70%. Price your Kindle book over $9.99 and Amazon drops that royalty to 35%. It's incredibly frustrating, but a factor to keep in mind when setting your price.

As a reminder, readers aren't nearly as price sensitive with nonfiction as they are with fiction. Romance novel readers, for example, tend to consume books like candy and therefore seek out titles priced at $2.99 or less. But if you want to learn how to train for a marathon, balance hormones, become a master marijuana gardener, or raise a family of pet pigs, you will quickly spend $9.99 without much thought. Guess what? So will your readers!

AUDIOBOOK PRODUCTION AND DISTRIBUTION

Audiobooks were once delivered on cassette tapes, and then later in CD boxed sets. They were expensive. There were local retailers who would sometimes allow you rent them just like videos on VHS tapes (remember those?). And then CDs went the way of vinyl records and have since become decorative coasters.

Today the largest retailer for audiobooks is Audible, which, not surprisingly, is owned by Amazon. Most Audible users pay an annual subscription rate and obtain credits for downloading a certain number of audiobook titles each year, or they can purchase audiobooks individually at prices ranging from around $10 to $40.

Today there are two primary providers of audiobooks to Audible and other online retailers: ACX and Findaway Voices.

Audiobook Creation Exchange (ACX): acx.com

Amazon acquired this independent audiobook production service several years ago, which means that its services favor Audible, but you can also opt to distribute your audiobook to iTunes.

Here's how it works: you can browse a directory of voice talent and listen to sample clips in order to find a narrator for your book, or you can upload your own pre-recorded and formatted audio files.

When you hire a narrator, you either pay a flat project fee (between $1,000 and $2,000, depending on the length of the book) or you offer a revenue split with the voice talent (hint: most prefer a flat fee). The fee you pay includes recording your audiobook and editing of all files so they meet ACX's quality standards and are ready to publish. You can use this service and set up distribution to Audible, Amazon, and iTunes all within a couple of weeks.

ACX Royalty Structure

Audible currently sets the pricing of your audiobook based on its length:

- Under 1 hour: less than $7

- 1 to 3 hours: $7 to $10

- 3 to 5 hours: $10 to $20

- 5 to 10 hours: $15 to $25

- 10 to 20 hours: $20 to $30

- Over 20 hours: $25 to $35

You will also have the option of granting Amazon/Audible exclusive or non-exclusive distribution rights. Exclusive rights mean you cannot distribute your audiobook elsewhere (such as iTunes, libraries, or schools) and in exchange for the exclusivity, you will earn a 40% royalty on audiobook sales. If you choose non-exclusive, that royalty rate drops to 25%.

Note that one popular way to earn more from your Audible sales is to participate in their "bounty" program. When you promote your audiobook and someone signs up for a new Audible subscription based on your recommendation, using a trackable affiliate link, you will earn a $50 bounty (finder's fee) for each new subscriber. If you convert a significant number of new Audible subscribers, those bounty fees can add up.

Self-Produced Audiobooks

If you want to record your audiobook yourself, keep in mind that the required file quality standards are incredibly high. There cannot be any background noise, static, or other miscellaneous sounds in your recording. You also have to prepare and edit the files according to Audible's guidelines. This means that you may need to set up a recording studio in your home and purchase a professional microphone and editing software.

Another way to produce your own recording is to hire a local recording studio to provide you with the equipment needed to record properly, as well as the editing services to prepare your files for distribution. Once you're done, you can set up your ACX account, upload your files, and become an official audiobook publisher.

Findaway Voices: findaway.com/findaway-voices

The other top player in audiobook production and distribution is Findaway Voices. This service also offers a directory of voice talent where you can listen to sound clips and hire someone to record your book. Unlike ACX, however, you cannot currently provide your own recording files.

But one big advantage that Findaway Voices brings is wider distribution. You can make your audiobook available through the following retailers:

- Amazon/Audible

- Apple iTunes

- Google

- Barnes and Noble Nook

- Baker and Taylor (library market)

- Playster

- Scribd

- Otto Radio

- InstaRead

- OverDrive (library market)

- Audiobooks.com

- And many more . . .

Findaway Voices pays authors 80% of the royalties it receives. The company also has a partnership with Smashwords, so if you're using them to distribute ebooks, you can use your Smashwords dashboard to access audiobook publishing services.

 PRO TIP: *Create multiple book formats.*

The more formats you put your book in, the more ways people can buy and consume it. Keep this in mind as you build your publishing plan. Your paperback book can also have a special edition hardcover, ebook, and audiobook. If you're extra adventurous, you could also create a companion workbook and/or adult coloring book.

"There will be obstacles. There will be doubters. There will be mistakes. But with hard work, there are no limits."

—Michael Phelps

CHAPTER 13
BESTSELLERS LISTS AND BOOK PREORDERS

Getting featured on the *New York Times* Best Sellers List is a big goal for many authors, but unfortunately not an easy one to accomplish, especially when self-published. The coveted list is compiled each week based on sales in certain brick-and-mortar bookstores plus *some* online book sales.

The *New York Times* acknowledges that its list is curated based on stores it selects and not based on total units sold. This means that even though a book might sell 5,000 to 10,000 copies in a week (the average number of sales needed to appear on the list), if the newspaper doesn't deem the title worthy of its list, it won't appear. Unfortunately, this has happened to several self-published titles, which demonstrates what some view as a rather elitist approach by the paper.

One way self-published authors could previously circumvent the bestsellers list requirements was to focus on ebook sales. However, in 2017 the *New York Times* removed several categories from its lists, including nonfiction ebooks (as well as fiction ebooks, young adult books, mass-market paperbacks, and several other categories). This is unfortunate since we had previously celebrated as numerous self-published authors reached *New York Times* bestseller status with their ebook sales.

Unfortunately, the outlook for self-published authors who want to reach the *New York Times* list is bleak without exceptional bookstore distribution, a hefty promotion plan, and perhaps a starring role on a reality TV show. (*Survivor* or *Real Housewives*, anyone?)

With that said, we've compiled some additional information on the various bestsellers lists and what it takes to get there. You also never know when the rules might change, so let's hope that the stigma for self-published books continues to improve.

WALL STREET JOURNAL (WSJ)

While not necessarily as prestigious as *The New York Times*, the WSJ bestsellers list is easier to reach because it's tabulated based on total units sold across all retailers, as reported by Nielsen BookScan (the industry standard in tracking book sales calculations). If you want your book to reach the WSJ list, especially if you've authored a business book, aim to sell 3,000 to 5,000 copies in a week. (Yes, it's daunting, but it's the reality.)

Note that sales must be acquired one book at a time. Bulk sales do not count, so ordering hundreds or even thousands of copies of your own book won't work. A better bet is to enlist thousands of family members, friends, clients, and social media followers to purchase copies of your book, one or two copies at a time.

USA TODAY

This list used to be compiled much like the WSJ list, based on total book sales in print and digital formats combined, but today it's a curated list, much like *The New York Times*. Even worse, categories aren't listed so total sales fall under one primary list.

PUBLISHERS WEEKLY

This is more of an insider list for the publishing industry, but like the WSJ list, it's compiled based on total book sales as reported by Nielsen BookScan. The upside of this list is that publishing industry professionals, including literary agents and editors from major publishing houses, pay close attention to this list. They're always on the lookout for promising self-published authors, so if your book makes it onto this list, you could end up on the radar of some important publishing pros.

AMAZON "BESTSELLER" LISTS

Many authors have a goal of getting their books on Amazon's various bestseller lists. Amazon has hundreds, if not thousands, of book categories and sub-categories, and because book sales are tabulated hourly, it's not difficult for a book to end up in the top ten of titles within a small sub-category on the site.

Unfortunately, this approach has eroded the term "bestselling author," because all it takes is convincing everyone you know to buy your book on a single day. Do this well and voilà! You can end up on a so-called bestseller list.

Stephanie worked with an author several years back who spent thousands of dollars hiring a company to hold an Amazon bestseller campaign for the launch of her financial advice guide. The company she hired reportedly enlisted dozens of other authors to announce the book to their networks via email and social media on launch day, with the goal of driving sales to Amazon.

As the day went on, the book moved up the ranks until it reached the #2 position in its tiny sub-category:

Books > Computers & Technology > Networking & Cloud Computing > Cloud Computing

That afternoon, the author called Stephanie to ask how many books had sold so far, and if she could write a big fat check to her favorite charity, as she had planned.

Guess how many copies sold that day? A grand total of 30 books.

The company that the author had paid thousands of dollars to probably bought at least half of the copies (15 copies x $20 = $300, less than 10% of the author's investment in those services), and the author's friends probably bought the other half. After the initial launch day, the book fell back off the top of the category list, and never landed there again.

Should you host an Amazon bestseller campaign?

While generating sales on a single day can potentially get your book in the top 10 list of a sub-category on Amazon, there is virtually no long-term value. Once the promotion is over, books fall right off the list unless the author keeps the promotion wheels in motion.

The exceptions to this rule are Top New Releases on Amazon and the Amazon Top 100 Bestsellers. If your book lands on either of these lists, it can help to boost sales just from the exposure alone. But don't expect to stay there without ongoing promotional effort.

If you want your book to make it to Amazon's Top 100 list, plan to sell at least 500 copies in a single day. And if you want to make the Top 10 list for the site, plan to generate at least 2,000 sales in a single day.

Amazon also pays attention to buyers so you won't be able to game the system. Don't bother ordering 500 copies of your book because that bulk purchase won't count. And don't bother creating dozens of Amazon accounts and ordering your books that way either. Amazon tracks IP addresses and credit cards and won't count those orders.

There is nothing wrong with having a great book launch and coming out of the gate with a solid promotional campaign. Whether you make it to a bestsellers list or not, you'll certainly gain some satisfaction from a job well-done. And hopefully, you'll also rack up some book reviews, too.

We also urge you to focus on long-term marketing for your book, not just the first few days after its release. Ongoing efforts will have much more meaningful results, allowing you to increase visibility and awareness for your book for weeks, months or even years. And yes, you can still make it on to a bestseller list on Amazon. But perhaps rather than hoping to land there long enough to order a latte at your favorite coffee shop, you could set a goal of getting on the list and *staying there for a while.* Ongoing promotion effort is the best way to make that happen!

BOOK PRE-ORDERS

While the bestsellers lists may not be your primary focus after what you've just read, there are still plenty of reasons to launch your book with as much momentum as possible. A strong book launch campaign can have many benefits:

- Generate word-of-mouth

- Rack up book reviews

- Get the attention of industry pros (literary agents and editors), potential clients, peers, media, and anyone else you want to impress

- Put some money in the bank

- Bring new life to backlist titles (previous books you've authored will usually get a boost after a new book release)

- Introduce readers to your other products and services

- Give you a reason to reach out to your networks and get people engaged

One of the best ways to hold a solid book launch is to accumulate pre-orders. IngramSpark and Lightning Source both allow authors to make their print books available for preorder on Amazon weeks or even months in advance of the planned book release date. Oddly, Amazon's KDP doesn't currently offer this feature.

When you put your book up for pre-sale on Amazon, customers can place their orders in advance of the launch date, and their payments won't be processed until the book is officially available. All pre-orders will count toward total book sales on launch day, so if you're focused on reaching any of the bestseller lists previously discussed, including Amazon's, this strategy can be helpful.

A pre-order campaign can also help generate reviews quickly since you will have built anticipation with readers and they will receive the book as soon as it's available and be anxious to crack it open. In addition, pre-orders can help your book appear on various book category lists on Amazon, so if you keep up your marketing efforts, it's possible you can remain on some lists for an extended period of time.

In order to set your book up for pre-orders with IngramSpark or Lightning Source, you'll need to have your book files ready to print. They require that both your cover and interior files are loaded and print-ready. This means you'll need to plan your pre-sale campaign into your book-publishing timeline.

You can host a pre-sale campaign for any length of time you like. We recommend no more than a few weeks, though, in order to keep your audience engaged and excited about the release.

EBOOK PRE-ORDERS

In addition to setting up your print book for pre-sale, you can also accept pre-orders for your Kindle and ebook editions. Pre-orders for Kindle should be set up directly via kdp.amazon.com. We also use and recommend Smashwords for pre-orders on the other ebook platforms including Apple iBooks, Barnes and Noble Nook, and Kobo.

Sales accumulated prior to launch day will count on the individual retailer's bestseller lists, so you could get listed on Amazon, Apple iBooks, Kobo, and Barnes and Noble as a bestseller that week—and that exposure can potentially generate even more sales.

Smashwords recommends launching your pre-order campaign at least four weeks in advance to create merchandising opportunities with retailers. For example, each week Apple promotes its top-selling pre-orders, and getting your book listed here could inspire more sales. Smashwords also recommends that for authors with previously published titles, you should update the back matter of your previous ebooks to indicate the on-sale date for your new book. This will not only help readers find your new title, but it may help retailers cross-promote your new ebook with buyers of your previous ebooks.

Note that Amazon Kindle requires that you have a fully formatted ebook file uploaded in order to participate in pre-orders. Smashwords allows authors at any stage, whether with a completed file or an "asset-less" pre-order, to schedule a pre-order campaign up to a full year in advance!

"*Just write every day of your life. Read intensely. Then see what happens. Most of my friends who are put on that diet have very pleasant careers.*"

—Ray Bradbury

AUTHOR INTERVIEW

Name: Honorée Corder

Book titles:
You Must Write a Book: Boost Your Brand, Get More Business and Become the Go-To Expert
The Prosperous Writer book series
The Miracle Morning book series

Website: honoreecorder.com

Can you tell us about your publishing journey and why you chose to self-publish your book?

I've published over 50 books, including multiple series.

I was encouraged by Mark Victor Hansen to write my first book. He told me, "Everyone is a coach and a speaker, you must write a book!" I took a popular keynote and turned it into my first book, *Tall Order! Master Strategies for Explosive Business Growth.* As I didn't have a college degree and had never taken a writing class, it never occurred to me to try the traditional path. I had a couple of colleagues (James Malinchak and Jeffrey

Gitomer) who had self-published with great success, and so that's the path I chose.

All of these years later, I wouldn't trade my self-published status for anything in the world! I enjoy complete creative and time freedom and control over my finished books.

What kind of business are you in and how has your book helped to grow your business?

Originally, I was a business and executive coach and used *Tall Order!* to generate leads and establish credibility. Today, I work with high-level business professionals and even celebrities to help them design, write, publish, launch and market their books (as well as turn them into multiple streams of income).

What have been some book marketing strategies that have generated the best results for you?

Being a guest on hundreds of podcasts has increased brand and book discoverability.

Giving away two free chapters of all of my books has increased not only my list but also my book sales.

A new book always increases the sales of my backlist.

Is there anything you would do differently for your next book? Any hard lessons learned?

I do something different and better with each book. My goal is to make every book indistinguishable from traditional publishing, so if someone has a bias against self-publishing, they'll take the risk because it is so well done.

I've learned almost *every* hard lesson (and I'm still learning with each book)! Typos on one of my first book's back covers resulted in the most expensive bonfire ever (seriously, I had a fire pit in my backyard and burned $3,500 worth of books). At least I was warm!

What advice would you offer to new authors?

Basically, publish your book well. Waiting, if you must, to have the money to invest in quality service providers (editors, proofreaders, formatters, cover designers, copywriters) before you publish. You'll never regret doing it well; I've been extremely embarrassed when I cut corners and realized it (or it was pointed out to me).

> *"People who are crazy enough to think they can change the world, are the ones who do."*
>
> —Steve Jobs

CHAPTER 14
ENDORSEMENTS AND BOOK REVIEWS

In the months before your book is published, you should begin reaching out to fellow authors to request endorsements. Ideally, testimonials should come from authors in your field, and the more well-known the author is, the better for building credibility with potential readers.

While you may think that big-name authors are untouchable, that hasn't been our experience. Many authors know that endorsing a book enhances their own marketing efforts since they gain added visibility with the readers of the books they endorse. And the fact is that it never hurts to ask. All they can do is say no, but they just might surprise you and say yes!

The key to getting the attention of well-known authors is to show up like a pro. Avoid telling them your whole life story or pleading for help. Also, please don't rant about how this is your first book, you're self-publishing, and you have no idea if anyone will ever buy your work. Seriously, some new authors do this and it does not inspire good results.

Contact information for even the biggest authors is almost always available. Search their websites or reach out via social media direct message. You'd be surprised by who reads their own messages on Facebook and LinkedIn. You might also ask author friends if they happen to know any top authors in your genre. Personal introductions can only help your case.

Here's a sample request for an endorsement that you can send out via email:

- - - - - - - - - - - - - -

Hi <author name>,

I loved your book <title> and found it enlightening because . . . <briefly explain>

I have a new book coming out this winter: <title>. It's about <brief description, just two or three sentences>. I am in the process of gathering endorsements for the jacket. Would you consider providing a testimonial? I would be happy to send you sample chapters or the entire manuscript for review—whatever you prefer. Having your support would mean a lot to me.

Thanks very much for your consideration.
Warm wishes,
<your name>
<your website link so he/she can see you're a pro>

- - - - - - - - - - - - - -

Note that complimenting the author's work demonstrates that you are a fan of their work and creates instant rapport (flattery will get you everywhere). Be sure to write two or three of the most compelling sentences you can muster about your book and why readers are going to love it.

If you have a large social media following, blog readership, or mailing list—basically an established platform—mention this as well so that the author understands he will receive additional exposure with your audience. You might add an additional sentence like this:

My social media accounts and mailing list combined reach over 30,000 people, and we have a solid marketing campaign planned so you'll definitely receive some great exposure.

If you don't yet have much of a platform, leave this out.

Once you land your first well-known author endorsement, mention it in your subsequent requests for endorsements. You can add something like this:

When you endorse my book, you'll be in good company. Oprah Winfrey has already contributed her endorsement. (Side note: Wouldn't that be amazing?!)

Also, if you've ever met the author or attended one of their events, mention this as well. Any time you can establish a personal connection can only help your case. In fact, if you really want a specific author to endorse your book, figure out how to attend one of her events and try to cross paths (not in a stalker-y way, of course). Even if you never get to meet in person, you can say you were there. And perhaps you'll get lucky and end up in an elevator together.

This happened to Stephanie when she traveled to another state to attend an event where one of her favorite authors was speaking. Not only did they make a personal connection after stepping onto an elevator together, he later endorsed her book and they ended up working on a project together. It's amazing what can happen when you set an intention and show up!

PRO TIP: *Timing is everything.*

Authors who have been on the *New York Times* Best Sellers list in the past year are probably in high demand and will be least likely to respond. But authors who were on the list several years ago, or who are top in the genre but have never made the list, will likely be more accessible. Spread your reach out to A-list, B-list, and C-list authors. You can never have too many endorsements.

When should you start seeking endorsements?

The best time to begin reaching out with endorsement requests is after the first round of editing is complete and you feel confident that the manuscript is in good shape. It's perfectly fine to send a version of the manuscript that still needs *some* editing—just let them know you're sending a manuscript that hasn't yet been fully edited.

You want to show your best work, so be sure you've had at least one round of professional editing completed before you start sending out requests.

What happens after you reach out?

Ideally you will receive responses to your email requests within a few days. Some authors may ask for the full manuscript, though others may just want to see a table of contents and a few sample chapters so they know you can write. We're sorry to report that the vast majority will not take time to read your book from cover to cover. Don't take this personally—it's just the way it works. We're all busy and have to prioritize our time.

Some may ask for you to send over some sample testimonials. That's right, they will ask you to write a few examples that they can choose from! They may change a word or two around, but for the most part you will be crafting your own endorsement. This is a reality in this business, so it's a good idea to have a few samples ready to go.

The bottom line is that endorsements can absolutely enhance the credibility of a book so don't be afraid to pursue them with gusto. Make a list of ten to twenty authors and start asking. With any luck, you'll end up with so many testimonials that you'll need to add a page or two to the beginning of your book to accommodate them.

HOW TO OBTAIN A FOREWORD

The foreword for a book is a short introduction to the work and a testimonial for the author. A foreword should be written by a well-known author or industry influencer. For example, if you're authoring a book about technology, Bill Gates would be a great person to write the foreword. On the flip side, the CEO of an unknown software company wouldn't likely add much value to the book, unless your target audience is familiar with that CEO.

In fact, corporate executives only make sense if they are truly well known by your target audience. The same is true for other professionals—attorneys, scientists, teachers, doctors. Unless they have some name recognition or their endorsement advances your credibility in some way, it's best to focus on well-known authors in your genre.

A foreword is totally optional, and unless you have a personal relationship with a top author, they aren't easy to get. Asking an experienced author to provide a three-sentence endorsement of your book is one thing but asking them to write a multi-page foreword—which means they have to read your complete manuscript first—is a lot to ask.

A foreword will come down to personal relationships. If this is important to you, go out and form a relationship long before your manuscript is written.

HOW TO GENERATE BOOK REVIEWS

Book reviews are essential because they help potential readers make a purchase decision. Sending out copies for potential review is something every author should include in their marketing plans. The more people who know about your book, the better the chance of building word-of-mouth buzz. If you want to take this seriously, plan to send out 50 to 500 review copies (or more) in both print and digital formats.

Following is a comprehensive list of book review sources, including both free and paid options.

A note on paid options: We do NOT advocate paid services that promise to churn out X number of manufactured (fake) reviews based on how much money you spend with them. However, we have included reputable services that offer quality reviews from real readers.

FREE BOOK REVIEW OPTIONS

Industry Bloggers – Seek out bloggers who cover topics of interest to your target audience or industry. For example, if you write about living a gluten-free lifestyle, find bloggers who cover food allergies, healthy diet advice, etc. Next, see if the bloggers conduct book reviews, publish book excerpts, or interview authors. Use Google searches to compile a list of bloggers to contact. Your searches might look like this:

- <genre> + "book review"

- <genre> + "author interview"

- <genre> + "book excerpt"

 PRO TIP: *Get better results with Google searches.*

When you put a search term in quotes, Google returns results that exactly match that phrase. So, if you want to search for "how to bake a cake," you won't get results that only have the word "cake."

You can also generate alternative results using the OR command like this: *business "book review" or "author interview."*

Book Review Bloggers – Bloggers have tremendous influence with readers when it comes to reviewing and recommending books. See the following directories to find bloggers who review books in your genre.

- The Book Blogger List: bookbloggerlist.com

- The Indie View: theindieview.com/indie-reviewers

- Book Page: bookpage.com/reviews

- My Book Pick: mybookpick.com (focuses on Indian authors)

- Emerald City Book Reviews: emeraldcitybookreview.com/reviews-by-genre

- Aussie Reviews: aussiereviews.com/category/nonfiction (for Australian authors)

- The Book Wheel: thebookwheelblog.com/reviews/genres/non-fiction (special focus on politics, nonfiction, memoir)

- The Bibliofile: the-bibliofile.com

- Bookstoker: bookstoker.com/genre/non-fiction

- Rated Reads: ratedreads.com

- Goodreads Book Bloggers groups: (search Goodreads.com for options)

- To purchase a list of 200+ nonfiction book bloggers, visit bit.ly/nonfictionreviewblogs.

Major Media Bloggers – All of the major magazines and newspapers now host blogs, from *The New York Times* to *Cat Fancy* magazine, and many of those blog posts are written by freelance contributors. Seek out freelancers who cover topics related to your target audience and offer up a review copy.

Email Subscribers – Periodically send a note to your mailing list subscribers gently reminding them that book reviews help sell books and that you'd greatly appreciate it if they would post a review for your book.

Midwest Book Review – A wonderful organization that supports indie authors, Midwest Book Review has been around for years and reviews printed books for free: midwestbookreview.com.

Smaller Publications – Don't overlook trade association newsletters and magazines, plus smaller magazines and even hometown newspapers.

Your Website – Create a "Review Copy Request" form on your website. Ask visitors to provide you with details, including website link and size of audience, in order to qualify to receive a complimentary review copy.

Contest on Your Site – Consider using Rafflecopter.com, a simple program that you can plug into your site to host a book giveaway contest—it's free! Gently ask (and remind) contest winners to post reviews after reading.

Online Groups – Announce that you are interested in sending out review copies to groups that reach your target audience. You can find all kinds of groups via Facebook, LinkedIn, Yahoo Groups, Goodreads, and BookRix.com. Be sure to get permission from the group moderator first.

Book Clubs – Offering your book to book clubs for free can be a great way to generate reviews and buzz. Search for book clubs by genre online and via Meetup.com. See also: From Left to Write (fromlefttowrite.com/information-for-publishers-and-authors/) and Book Club Reading List (bookclubreading.com/submit-your-book/).

Noise Trade – This site allows you to list your ebook as a free giveaway for any length of time you choose. In exchange, readers provide their email addresses, which you can download for follow-up. They can also give a "tip" for authors, resulting in small fees potentially earned for books listed on NoiseTrade.com.

Social Media – Invite your audience to become book reviewers. You can share a link to your "Review Copy Request" form on your website or conduct a contest to give away several review copies. You can also start early and build a waiting list for reviewers well before your book is published!

Giveaways at Events – Whenever you donate copies of your book for raffle prizes or gifts, include a note asking the recipient for a review.

Review Communities – There are numerous communities where writers can share their work and get feedback. This is a great way to build some interest and create fans *before* your book is published: Wattpad.com, WeBook.com.

Book Life – You can submit your book for free review consideration at BookLife.com, hosted by *Publishers Weekly*.

PAID BOOK REVIEW OPTIONS

NetGalley – For a modest fee, you can apply to list your book in the NetGalley.com directory and make it available for their 300K reviewers to choose from.

Kirkus – An established and reputable company, Kirkus.com provides professional-level reviews for a modest fee.

Goodreads Giveaways – More than 40,000 people enter to win books from Goodreads Giveaways each day. Authors can offer up books for free to this program and specify the number of days the promotion will run (they recommend 30 days). An average of 825 people enter to win these promotions, and Goodreads selects the winners at the end and sends authors a CSV file with addresses. When mailing copies of books to winners, be sure to insert a note requesting that the recipient write a review if they enjoy the book. Similar giveaway sites: LibraryThing.com, BookLikes.com.

Note that if your book is enrolled in Amazon's KDP Select program, you will not be able to participate in free ebook give-aways with non-Amazon sites (a major downside of the Kindle exclusive distribution clause).

Foreword Magazine – Reputable reviews for indie authors via Forewordreviews.com.

BookBub – The top service for paid email campaigns to promote books via BookBub.com. Also BookSends.com. Both may result in additional reviews.

Author Buzz – Get book announcements out to libraries, bloggers, book clubs and more via AuthorBuzz.com.

Bargain Booksy – If your ebook is priced for sale between $.99 and $4.99, you can purchase an email promotion to members on BargainBooksy.com. See also FreeBooksy.com.

START SOMEWHERE – YOU DON'T HAVE TO DO IT ALL

We realize this is a lot of information and it may seem overwhelming—it's a lot for us to think about, too! For book reviews, and anything related to marketing your books, know that you don't have to do it *all*. But you do have to start somewhere. Perhaps pick a few of the book review sources listed and simply get started. You can also spread out the effort over time.

Don't let this overwhelm you! Find a way to make market-ing your book a fun task. And if marketing simply feels like a painful activity for you, then at least keep track of your "wins" and celebrate those so that you don't dread these essential tasks completely. Remember, if you want people to read your book, you've got to help your audience find your book.

 PRO TIP: *Get in the habit of asking for reviews.*

As an author, you can expect that your readers will periodically contact you, either via email or social media, to let you know they enjoyed your book. When this happens, always reply with gracious appreciation and ask the reader to post a review online. This may sound like a no-brainer, but it's easy to forget when you're basking in the glow of flattery.

Fun Fact

A 6x9 trade paperback has an average of 250 words per page. Use this number to estimate page count based on the length of your manuscript.

CHAPTER 15
NAVIGATING AMAZON

Like it or not, we all have to put focused effort and attention into selling on Amazon and understanding how it works, since the majority of book sales happen there. Many independent authors have a love-hate relationship with Amazon due to some of their policies.

Think of Amazon as a giant search engine, which is exactly how most people use the site. For example, when you type in a search for "book on divorce" or "book about gardening in Iowa," Amazon returns what it deems to be the most relevant results. And those results are based on technology called *algorithms*.

Though Amazon doesn't publicly share how its algorithms calculate search results, those of us who've been around for a while have come to our own conclusions based on what we've seen and experienced. It's widely believed that Amazon's algorithms look at keywords, number of reviews, number of sales, recent sales activity, click-through rates, and more. Keep reading for more details.

KEYWORDS

When you set up your book for distribution, you will have the ability to identify specific keyword phrases that describe your book (also known as "metadata"). Consider what terms your target audience would use to find your book. Also, incorporate top keywords into your book's title or subtitle for best results. Choose keywords carefully, as they can have a big impact on search results. You can also test different keyword combinations later in the Kindle dashboard if needed.

I just searched Amazon for "guide to running" and these are the top results, in order as they appear:

- *The Young Entrepreneur's Guide to Starting and Running a Business*

- *Relentless Forward Progress: A Guide to Running Ultramarathons*

- *The Butler's Guide to Running the Home and Other Graces*

- *Running Randomized Evaluations: A Practical Guide*

- *Legal Guide to Starting and Running a Small Business*

Clearly Amazon's algorithms aren't smart enough to understand that "running" is the focused topic in that search phrase. It's possible that this eclectic list of search results may have also factored in previous search history since I read business books; it's hard to know for sure. But let this serve as a warning that *keywords matter.*

Also note that you can incorporate keyword phrases into the description for your book, too, and you should. But the most important keywords belong in your book's title and/or subtitle.

CATEGORIES

The categories where your book is listed can have a major impact on sales. For example, if your book is about running marathons, but it isn't listed in the running category, it will potentially miss out on traffic from people who browse that category.

When you publish with Amazon you indicate suggested categories for your book based on BISAC codes (see Chapter 8), but ultimately Amazon chooses its own categories for you, which don't always exactly align with BISAC codes. If you find your book is not assigned to the proper category, try changing the category selection in the Kindle edition, which should also impact the print edition. If that doesn't work, don't be afraid to contact Amazon support and ask for the change. This is best accomplished via your Amazon Author Central account, which we will discuss shortly.

BOOK SALES HISTORY

Like any retailer, Amazon wants to make money, therefore it pays attention to what books are selling well and gives those titles higher priority over competing titles. The more book sales you generate, the more Amazon will help boost sales by cross-promoting your book with other titles and giving it a higher position in search results. Yes, this can be frustrating because it requires that you're driving sales yourself. But if you're doing the work and driving buyers to your book, Amazon will reward your efforts with increased promotion on the site.

ADDITIONAL FACTORS FOR AMAZON ALGORITHMS

Number of Book Reviews - Book reviews show Amazon that your book is popular and liked by readers, provided reviews are mostly positive. Some believe that reaching a certain number of reviews (between 70 and 90), actually triggers something within Amazon's algorithms that helps with sales. All we know for sure is that reviews influence potential readers to buy books, so your goal should always be to generate as many reviews as possible on an ongoing basis.

Note that a review from someone who purchased your book from Amazon is denoted as a "verified purchase" and holds more weight than other reviews, not just with Amazon, but with readers, too.

Click-Through Rates - Amazon tracks how many times a product appears in search results and how many times a user clicks on that product. If your book isn't generating enough clicks, that can impact future search results. This means that your book cover and title need to appeal to readers and inspire them to click through to your book page.

Conversion Rates - When someone clicks on your book and actually follows through to make the purchase, that is considered a conversion. When you have a higher conversion rate for book sales, Amazon will factor this in. And when visitors to your book page don't buy, Amazon notices this, too. You can help by ensuring you have an excellent book description, professional cover design, editorial reviews, and author bio.

Search History - Amazon also looks at the past history of the buyer to decide on results, which may explain why when I searched "guide for running," I received several results about small business. Therefore, the search results you receive for a key phrase can vary from the results your sister gets.

The bottom line is that you can't control how Amazon displays your book in search results, but you can certainly help the process by following the tips we've just shared.

HOW AMAZON CALCULATES SALES RANKING FOR BOOKS

Every book on Amazon has a sales rank number located near the publisher information. This rating indicates how well the book is selling at that moment in time. It may seem counterintuitive, but the lower the sales rank, the more copies of the book have sold that day.

As an author, it's helpful to monitor sales trends for your books, especially if you have active marketing and publicity campaigns. If an article comes out about you in an industry magazine or you're a featured guest on a radio show, your book's sales rank can show a resulting spike in sales. (Or not! Unfortunately, publicity doesn't always lead to book sales.)

Sales ranking is recalculated throughout the day, so the rank you see for your book at 9:00 A.M. will be different from its ranking at 5:00 P.M.

While Amazon doesn't publish information about how it tabulates book sales ranking numbers, many authors have speculated over the years about how the ranking system correlates to the number of copies sold based on our own experiences.

Following are *estimated* average book sales based on the ranking.

Sales Ranking vs. Number of Books Sold Per Day:

50,000 to 100k = **1 or fewer books per day**

10,000 to 50,000 = **2 to 10 books per day**

3,000 to 10,000 = **10 to 100 books per day**

500 to 3,000 = **100 to 200 books per day**

200 to 500 = **200 to 500 books per day**

35 to 200 = **500 to 1,000 books per day**

20 to 35 = **1,000 to 2,000 books per day**

10 to 20 = **2,000 to 3,000 books per day**

1 to 10 = **3,000+ books per day**

AMAZON ADVERTISING CAMPAIGNS

Just as Facebook made the shift to being a pay-to-play network, requiring paid advertising in order to get visibility for posts shared there, Amazon is clearly making a shift in the direction of pay-to-play for book marketing and visibility.

Using this model, Amazon earns money whether a browser buys a book or simply clicks on a sponsored title. It's another revenue-generating machine for the retail giant.

Sponsored books currently show up in the following places on Amazon:

- **The top of search results.** If you search for "diabetes cookbook" or "Vietnam war books," the first couple of results are usually sponsored titles.

- **In the middle of search results.** Not only do sponsored books appear at the top of search results, sponsored titles are also sprinkled throughout all search results. A sponsored book can be shown as the 7th or 15th or 30th book in the list of search results.

- **In the "Sponsored Products Related to this Item" section** on individual book sales pages.

- **On the right side of a book's page under the "Add to Cart" buttons.** (Product Display Ads)

- **On the lock screen and top of Kindle reader devices.** (Product Display Ads)

What does this mean for authors?

This shift toward pay-to-play advertising means that if you want your book to get more visibility on Amazon, you're going to have to pay for that exposure.

Amazon ads are currently rather inexpensive, costing an average of between $.10 and $.30 per click. So, if you optimize your ads to target the right potential readers, and if your book's sales page does a good job of converting visitors into buyers, then your small investment in product clicks could pay for itself big time.

The other good news is that advertising with Amazon is a rather low-risk proposition. You can set a daily budget of as little as $1 and then monitor the results.

Aiming for Return on Investment (ROI)

With any kind of advertising, the goal should be to generate a significant ROI. Ideally, for every dollar spent, you would earn back $2 or more in book sales.

For example, if you earn an average of $5 per book sold, and you spend $4 in click ads to generate one sale, you'd earn an ROI of $1 and come out ahead. Of course, the goal should be to earn a much higher return on investment, though any ROI is better than none at all!

For many nonfiction authors, it's not as much about the revenue earned as it is about getting the book into the hands of readers. Perhaps this means that you wouldn't mind spending $4 per sale because you'd still come out ahead and gain a new reader. You might even be willing to take a loss on ads because your book itself generates ROI from other business opportunities, such as speaking engagements or consulting clients.

I've heard from many authors utilizing Amazon ads. Some rave about their results and report generating lots of book sales thanks to their pay-per-click ads. Others have reported that results are mediocre at best. I haven't yet heard from anyone who found it to be a complete waste of time and money, though I'm sure there are some who haven't been as successful with them. As with any kind of marketing, you have to test to find out what works best for your unique product, or book in this case.

What are the options for advertising?
There are two primary types of Amazon Ads:

Product Display Ads show your book on another book's page of your choosing. For example, you can identify several competing book titles and set your ads to display on those books' pages.

Sponsored Product Ads show up during keyword searches. For example, you might set an ad to display whenever shoppers search for a competing author in your genre or when they search for a phrase like "how to run a marathon."

With either ad option, you only pay when a user clicks on your ad. For best results, we recommend setting budgets for both ad sets and then monitoring results. If your ROI is higher than your ad investment, then it makes sense to increase your advertising budget. So, if you spend $50 on ads and generate

$75 in book sales, your ROI is good. Try bumping up your budget to $100 or more to see if you can achieve even better results.

Also, advertising takes time. Give it a couple of months before you decide to throw in the towel on ads. Many nonfiction authors are seeing excellent results with Amazon ads, especially those with niche nonfiction titles.

To locate ads, go to kdp.amazon.com and click on the menu next to your book title. Click on "Promote and Advertise."

We've compiled an extensive report that gives step-by-step instructions for setting up your Amazon ads. Download a copy here: nonfictionauthorsassociation.com/reader-bonus.

AMAZON KDP SELECT PROGRAM

The KDP Select program is available to Kindle publishers, and enrolling requires that you give Amazon exclusive distribution rights to your ebook. This means that you cannot distribute your ebook via the Barnes and Noble Nook, iBookstore, Smashwords, etc. This is one of those policies that frustrate independent authors and publishers because it's Amazon's way of trying to control the ebook market.

The KDP Select program offers several options:

Price Promotions – This is one of the most popular KDP Select features because it allows authors to opt to make their Kindle ebooks available for free or at a low cost (Kindle Countdown Deals) for a brief period of time. This can be a useful strategy for fiction authors who write series books. Getting the first book in as many readers' hands as possible can lead to sales of other books in a series. For nonfiction authors, this program rarely holds much value, unless you have several titles and perhaps want to bring new life to an old title.

Kindle Unlimited and Kindle Lending Library – When you enroll your ebook in Kindle Unlimited and/or the Kindle Lending

Library, readers who participate in these programs can read your ebook for free. You will then be compensated based on the percentage of the book read out of a global fund that Amazon creates each month to compensate participating authors.

Payments earned with these programs are low, but Amazon claims that you can potentially reach more readers by participating. The theory is that readers who wouldn't otherwise find or purchase your book will be more likely to read it because they can access it for free with their Amazon Prime membership.

We feel this program better serves fiction authors who want to reach a bigger audience.

Royalties – The KDP Select program increases royalties earned on ebook sales in India, Brazil, and Mexico. Instead of earning 35% royalties, you'll earn 70%. This might matter to you if you generate an incredible number of sales in these countries, but that is rare.

Bottom line: The KDP Select program may work well for some fiction authors, but for nonfiction authors who carve out a niche, it won't likely bring enough benefits to make it worthwhile to give Amazon exclusive distribution rights to your ebook.

AMAZON AUTHOR CENTRAL: *Steps to Maximize Your Account*

Amazon's Author Central is an essential tool for managing your book(s) and author information on the site. Every author should take full advantage of the free service because it allows you to update content on your book page, keep author bio information up-to-date, see your sales data, and more. As soon as your book is available on Amazon, use the following steps to make sure you're utilizing all the benefits Author Central brings.

Claim Your Book
Once your book is published and available on Amazon (whether self-published or traditionally published, it works the same), go

to AuthorCentral.Amazon.com and log in with your existing Amazon user ID and password. (If you aren't already an Amazon customer, you'll need to create an account.)

Once there, click on the "Books" tab and then the button that says "Add Books." Follow the prompts to search for your book and then claim it for your author profile. Repeat these steps for your print and ebook editions.

Author Tab

Add the following elements to your author profile:

- **Biography** – This should be an overview of your professional experience as it relates to your book(s). One to five paragraphs is fine, and include your website link at the end. (A lot of authors forget to include their website—make this a habit anytime you share a biography publicly.)

- **Blog Feed** – If you're a blogger, be sure to include a link to your blog's RSS feed. Amazon will automatically feed your latest posts into your author page. If you don't know your feed address, try adding "/feed" to the end of your website URL like this:

  www.mywebsite.com/feed.

- **Photo** – Upload a professional author photo. This will be featured on your book's page on Amazon, and in search results for your name.

- **Videos** – If you have a video book trailer, a short video of you speaking, or another video under 500 MB in size, you can upload them here. (This is an optional feature.)

- **Twitter and Facebook** – If you're a Twitter and/or Facebook user, input links to your profiles here so that page visitors can follow you.

- **Events** – If you're hosting a book signing, speaking engagement, or other events, you can list them here.

- **Links** – Here you will also find a link to preview your author page, as well as the direct link to your author page so you can share it with others.

Books Tab

Here you will see your book(s) listed, including current sales rank and number of reviews for each of your books. Click on the book title to go the Editing page and add the following details (all will appear on the sales page for the book):

- **Editorial Reviews** – List credible reviews for your book from media sources or from fellow author testimonials you've gathered.

- **Product Description** – This is the sales copy for your book, often taken from the back cover. Here you can expand on your book description if you like. Be sure to include keywords in the description of your book (phrases you think readers would use to search for a book like yours).

- **From the Author** – Post an announcement or bit of news to potential readers. For example, "I'm honored to announce that my book received a gold book award from The Nonfiction Book Awards."

- **From the Inside Flap** – If you have a hardcover book, copy the data from the inside of your jacket here.

- **From the Back Cover** – If you used your back cover copy for your description, you do not need to repeat it here.

- **About the Author** – Amazon says this should be the length of a bio you would list on the back cover of your book (one paragraph). This is displayed below the description for your book on its sales page.

Important note when updating your book: At the top of the screen, to the right of your book image and publisher data,

Amazon will list whether the information is listed for the print edition or Kindle. Changes made to one will *not* populate to the other so you need to make changes on both.

Sales Info Tab

This tab allows you to monitor your book sales history. There are currently three options in the drop-down menu:

- **Nielsen BookScan** – Nielsen is the industry's leading source for tracking book sales from retailers beyond Amazon, including brick-and-mortar bookstores—though it admits to only capturing about 70% of print book sales from retailers outside of Amazon. However, we find that their tracking is fairly accurate for authors who sell most of their books online, and it's a good resource for monitoring sales activity. You can also view sales by geography so you can see the cities where you've generated the most sales and see a quick summary in the upper right corner of total sales in the last week.

- **Sales Rank** – The sales rank trends for your book(s) over time.

- **Author Rank** – Amazon calculates an author's rank, just as it calculates ranking for books. This feature shows your ranking over time. Note that if your overall author rank earns top-100 placement in a given category, Amazon will note this on your book's page.

Customer Reviews Tab

Here you will see a listing of all reviews of your book, which is extra helpful if you've authored multiple titles because you can check to see if new reviews have been posted. You may also want to contact past reviewers when you release your next book so that you can offer them review copies. This gives you a handy place to find them.

Overall, it's a good idea to pop into your Author Central account periodically so you can monitor sales activity and update details for your book and your author bio, which can change with time. Any time you release a new title, you'll need to repeat the above steps.

 PRO TIP: *Get in touch with Amazon customer service.*

Amazon has notoriously hard-to-reach customer service, but as an author, you'll have better access to support. From your Author Central account home page, scroll down to the very bottom of the page to the teeny tiny "Contact Us" link. This will allow you to send an email to Author Central support, and they can help with all kinds of issues related to your book. Also, here's a direct link (must be signed in): authorcentral.amazon.com/gp/help/contact-us.

AMAZON'S USED BOOK MARKETPLACE

Authors often wonder why their books appear on Amazon under the Used Books category, especially if the book has only recently been released. There are legitimate reasons for this.

Most books are distributed through Ingram, the world's largest supplier of books to bookstores. When new titles are released and available through Ingram, independent booksellers can offer them for sale, and purchase them at the wholesale discount you set for your book.

When your book is released into the wild, you will likely find it available for sale with many independent booksellers—across Amazon and even on independent bookseller websites. Unfortunately, that doesn't mean the booksellers have actually *purchased* your book—yet. If and when your book is sold, they will then purchase the book through Ingram and drop-ship it to the buyer. Yes, this means they can list your book for sale without actually having a single copy in inventory.

Many of these indie booksellers will attempt to beat Amazon's available retail price in hopes of capturing the sale. The good news is that regardless of who ends up selling your book, you are still compensated based on sales through the distributor (Ingram).

The Downside of the Used Book Marketplace

Copies of your book will likely end up being sold in Amazon's used book marketplace and there's nothing you can do about it. These copies may come from actual readers but can also come from the review copies you've sent out or submissions to award competitions. You won't be compensated for used book sales.

On the upside, you can think of used books like library books. Once a copy of your book is purchased by a library, it can be shared over and over again. Though you won't be paid by those borrowers, each reader can potentially become a fan who visits your website and invests in your other books, products, and services. Don't lose sleep at night over used book sales.

 PRO TIP: *Mark your review copies.*

Whenever you send out a review copy, be sure to stamp it: "Review Copy - Not for Resale." This is meant to prevent the book from being resold, and a simple rubber stamp can make this process easy (stamp the front cover *and* title page). Ethical booksellers will honor this and will not attempt to resell a review copy.

 **AUTHOR INTERVIEW**

Name: Blake Atwood

Book Titles:
The Gospel According to Breaking Bad
Don't Fear the Reaper: Why Every Author Needs an Editor

Website: blakeatwood.com

Can you tell us about your publishing journey and why you chose to self-publish your books?

Prior to writing *The Gospel According to Breaking Bad* in early 2013, I'd pitched it to a startup, digital-only publisher who expressed interest in the idea. Buoyed by their encouragement, I began writing the book in earnest. However, as I sent a few chapters to the publisher, their suggested revisions didn't mesh with my vision for the book. As no contract had been signed, I walked away from the opportunity.

By that time, knowing that I wanted to capitalize on *Breaking Bad's* immense popularity that year, I had no recourse but to self-publish in order to meet my preferred release date.

I published my book on the same day as the last season's premiere episode. Consequently, I enjoyed free press in both the *Washington Post* and the *Huffington Post* as my book rode on the coattails of a cultural fascination with the final plight of Walter White.

Ultimately, I chose self-publishing for its speed to market and the ability to control the content. At the time, I had also immersed myself in podcasts and articles touting self-publishing as the *only* smart path to choose these days. I drank the Kool-Aid and became an ardent proponent of self-publishing. (I've since become more moderate in my publishing views.)

Although the allure of traditional publishing still tugged at me—I often wished I would have had the idea for my book about two years before I began writing it—the payoffs of self-publishing have been immense, and I'm not just talking about sales, which were good the first year but inevitably tapered off.

I wrote and self-published that book while working at a full-time job. That book gave me the self-confidence I needed to write more books. In fact, that book opened doors I would have never been able to open myself. By walking through those doors, I was able to quit my job two years later and pursue writing, editing, and ghostwriting full-time, a freelancing position I still gratefully enjoy today—all thanks to Walter White.

I self-published my second book, *Don't Fear the Reaper: Why Every Author Needs an Editor*, because I wanted a short book as a business card. The book offers editing tips, advice on how to work with an editor, and how to overcome the need for validation as a writer.

Again, time to market and full control led my self-publishing decision.

What kind of business are you in and how has your book helped to grow your business?

I own BA Writing Solutions LLC, which means I write, edit, and ghostwrite full-time. My books have been of inestimable value to my business. To point would-be clients to my personal work provides proof of my services. My books certainly generate leads and establish my credibility.

Furthermore, I've been traditionally published as a co-author on *The Father Effect,* and I've helped authors pitch their work to traditional publishers. Having both self-publishing and traditional publishing experience allows me to offer that guidance to my clients.

What have been some book marketing strategies that have generated the best results for you?

- If your book is timely, launch it during the right window. I doubt I would have sold my first thousand copies of *The Gospel According to Breaking Bad* had I not released it while the show was at its peak popularity. Had I actually known what a launch team was back then, I imagine my sales would have multiplied.

- Work your connections, but don't be annoying. The only reason I was featured in national publications when my book came out was that I asked a journalist connection if she'd be interested in endorsing my book. Then *she* suggested writing an article about the show that would mention my book. That's a kindness I'll never be able to repay.

- Release new versions. This often helps breathe new life into older versions. For instance, I used ACX.com and created the audiobook version of *The Gospel According to Breaking Bad*. I used Babelcube.com to have it translated into Spanish. These new versions gave me the opportunity to talk about my book again without being the "Buy my book!" guy.

- Write guest posts for sites your target audience likely reads. For *Don't Fear the Reaper*, I guest posted at a dozen or more well-known websites for writers. While there's no telling if those posts led to sales, they did lead to *connections with influencers.* These guest posts also led to a monthly column about editing at TheWriteLife.com.

- Consider how you can repurpose content. Some of *Reaper* became my (now-defunct) podcast on editing tips, and some of that content has been reused as blog posts and teaching material. When you repurpose, you can always point back to the original source.

Is there anything you would do differently for your next book? Any hard lessons learned?

I'd give myself time and grace to get the right words on the page. I'd tell myself not to feel rushed, even though the rush of getting your words into the world is hard to keep at bay.

I'd be more cognizant of who my true audience might be.

I'd hire a book designer.

I'd create a launch team.

I'd have a marketing plan ready many months before launch.

I wouldn't look at my launch as the finish line.

What advice would you offer to new authors?

Don't rush your writing. Get the words to where you're 90 percent happy with them. No book is perfect. Then enlist help: beta readers, editor, designer, launch team, etc.

Hire an editor and a book designer. Like Steinbeck wrote in *Journal of a Novel,* "You can't train for something all your life and then have it fall short because you are hurrying to get it finished." Why invest months or years into writing your book and then *not* invest the money to ensure it's the best it can be?

Read about the craft. Join a writers group. Go to writing conferences. But don't let those activities replace actually *writing.* Commit to writing something *every day*—or, at least, every day you have time. Writers write! Are you a writer?

CHAPTER 16
YOUR WEBSITE AND ECOMMERCE STRATEGY

When developing a website, you may think you have two primary choices: a site for the book (booktitle.com) and a site for you as the author (authorname.com). But there is also a third option: a magazine-style site. Let's look at some of the pros and cons for each.

Author Site: If your goal is to brand yourself as an authority in your field, a professional speaker, and a media interview source, it makes sense to focus efforts on developing your personal brand, with your book being an *extension* of that brand. Having an author site creates a level of professionalism that lends itself to building your career as an author. (By the way, if your author name is taken, try AuthorAnnieSmith.com or AnnieSmithAuthor.com.)

Book Site: A book site can have its advantages, but if you plan to write more books in the future, then you'll be faced with managing multiple sites—and working to drive traffic to all those sites.

Magazine-Style Site: A magazine site should focus on your subject matter expertise. For example, if your book is about training dogs, you might create a site about dog care. Or, even better, you could narrow down your niche focus to elder dog care or large-breed dog care.

WHY MAGAZINE SITES RULE

Content is still king online and one of the best ways to attract website traffic is to consistently add content to your site via blogging. Each time you publish a new blog post, you give Google a reason to find your site.

Several years ago, a client asked Stephanie to write a blog post on how to autograph books. At first, Stephanie thought it was an unnecessary topic, but after thinking about the details involved in signing books at events, she wrote the post—and assumed it wouldn't be read by too many people. She never expected to be so wrong. Years later, that remains one of the most popular blog posts she's ever written for that site.

There are two lessons here: Each new blog post you write gets indexed by Google and gives the search engine another reason to bring visitors to your site. Also, you never know which content is going to take off. Sometimes it's an article you never expected would become popular. That blog post about autographing books attracted thousands of readers who wouldn't have otherwise found Stephanie's site.

If you want to drive traffic to your site, creating content on a regular basis is key. Once a visitor is on your site and likes the content he's just read by you, the goal is to get him to buy your book, sign up for your mailing list, or purchase your other books, products or services.

By the way, your site content can include blog posts, podcast recordings, videos, interviews with peers, product recommendations, book reviews, guest posts by industry friends, etc.

Here are some examples to consider:

If your book is a memoir about your experiences traveling through Europe, your site could focus on European travel tips. Or, you could narrow your focus to any of the following:

- European travel for baby boomers
- European travel for college students who want to study abroad
- Traveling through Europe on a budget
- Traveling to a specific city like Paris or London

If your book is a guide to living a happier life, you could focus on general happiness, or niche it down to any of the following:

- Happiness strategies for single moms
- How to be a happier teen
- How to raise happier kids
- How to be happier at work
- Finding happiness in retirement

If your book is about how to grow a business, choosing a niche would be wise, since there is a lot of competition in this space. You could try any of these ideas:

- How to grow a retail business
- Ways to start and grow a freelance graphic-design business
- How to grow a family-owned business
- How kids can start a business
- How to grow a business you can sell

Do you see how this works? Choosing to focus on a specific topic that is related to the books you write can help you build a platform *around* your area of expertise and then go well beyond the standard five-page author or book website.

Here are some additional examples to consider:

- A low-carb cookbook author who shares new recipes and cooking tips several times per week. (Imagine how well your new cookbooks will sell after you've been keeping your readers engaged with recipes they love!)

- A memoir writer who had success as a teen athlete and writes about healthy lifestyle tips for teen athletes.

- An author who covers leadership for millennial women, both in the blog and a book series.

- A fact-based site that shares details about the history of the state of Texas, where the author's books are historical guides that complement the website content.

- A technology-focused blog with tips on growing your IT business. This is what Karl does for his audience of IT consultants at SmallBizThoughts.com.

- Articles on how to write, publish, and promote nonfiction books. This is what Stephanie and her team do over at NonfictionAuthorsAssociation.com.

If you can commit to building the content, a magazine-style site is one of the best choices you can make in establishing yourself as an authority and attracting your ideal readers.

REAL-WORLD EXAMPLES OF MAGAZINE-STYLE SITES

- **CatBehaviorAssociates.com** – Run by author Pam Johnson-Bennett (whose excellent tagline is "America's Favorite Cat

Expert"), this site is loaded with all kinds of advice on caring for cats including behavior issues, dental health, nutrition, and much more.

- **DearDivorceCoach.com** – Cherie Morris is an attorney, divorce mediator, divorce coach, and author of the book *Should I Stay or Should I Go?* Her site offers video tips and blog posts to help men and women navigate the divorce process.

- **DrAxe.com** – The tagline for this site is "Food is medicine," and it's the brand-builder for its creator, Dr. Josh Axe, a certified doctor of natural medicine, chiropractor, and author. The site is loaded with articles covering natural remedies for all kinds of medical conditions, plus recipes, food reviews, and fitness advice. While this is a magazine-style site, it is branded with the author's domain name, which is not easy to accomplish, but can be done if you produce a LOT of content.

- **SixFigurePetSittingAcademy.com** – Author Kristin Morrison's site offers free advice for starting a pet-sitting business through blog posts and videos. Of course, you can also enroll in her programs or buy her books here too.

- **HuffingtonPost.com** – Started by Arianna Huffington as a political opinion site, HuffPost is the ultimate example of a magazine-style site. It expanded its coverage to all kinds of topics, enlisted thousands of writers, and grew to generate massive readership. The site was ultimately sold to AOL in 2011 for a reported $315 million. Yowza!

What about an author website?

Don't panic, but it may make sense to also have an author site where you can attract media interviews and speaking engagements. Many nonfiction authors have both a magazine site and author site because both bring their own unique value. We walk the talk and both maintain separate author sites: StephanieChandler.com and KarlPalachuk.com.

WEBSITE DESIGN

The good news is that it's easier than ever to have a website designed, and it doesn't have to cost a fortune. While there are do-it-yourself options out there, if you have any kind of a budget, we strongly recommend investing in professional website design. For as little as $500, you can have a top quality WordPress site designed. Ask around for designer recommendations or hire a designer through a freelance labor site like Upwork.com.

PRO TIP: Save on website design.

You can save big money on website design by purchasing an inexpensive WordPress template from a site like themeforest.net or templatemonster.com. Next, hire a website designer to install and customize your template. You can save time and money on website development by using a template, and your site can look incredibly professional as a result.

WEBSITE DOMAINS

It is essential that you register your own website domain name so that you can direct your audience to your own real estate on the internet. Your site should not be part of a bigger network, like Blogger.com. There is nothing inherently wrong with free blog networks; however, you're building a business and your site identity should be as professional as possible.

Domain names can be purchased from many sources. Karl prefers Network Solutions (networksolutions.com) because they're a big operation and have been around for a long time. Stephanie prefers GoDaddy (godaddy.com) for domain registration because it's easy to use and cost-effective. Either way you go, domain registration is inexpensive (averaging around $15 per year).

When choosing the domain name for your website, it's best to stick with the standard ".com" extensions. While new extensions are being introduced every day, most people are in the habit of typing in ".com." If you choose ".net" or ".biz" and you have a competitor with the ".com" site extension, you will undoubtedly lose site visitors to them.

Also, avoid putting dashes, numbers or erroneous words in your domain name. It may be harder to find shorter domain names these days, but it's worth the effort to try and find a descriptive name that isn't too long and is also memorable. You can try many word combinations until you find something that works just right for you.

You may also want to register additional domain names for marketing purposes. This includes variations on your site name. For example, Karl has a site focused on healthy living to create success at RelaxFocusSucceed.com. He also registered the domain Relaxfocus**and**succeed.com, which redirects to his main site, in case a potential user types it in incorrectly.

Domain names can also be forwarded. For example, you could register the domain name for your book title (myawesomebook.com) and share that link as part of your book launch campaign, but have the domain forwarded to a book page on your magazine-style site or your author site. Domain forwards are easy to set up from your domain host and don't cost anything beyond the standard domain registration fee.

WEBSITE HOSTING

A website host manages the server where your website resides, and you'll pay a monthly or annual fee for hosting. Both GoDaddy and Network Solutions also sell website hosting, email hosting, and even website templates. You can host your sites with either of these companies or another host like ServInt.com (Stephanie's choice for hosting provider), BlueHost.com, or any number of available website hosting services.

Where your site is hosted isn't a huge consideration when you're starting out, since most hosting services operate and cost about the same. But as your site grows and traffic increases, you'll want to be sure you're with a host that offers excellent technical support, data backups, and redundancy (if the server goes down, another server takes over immediately).

A high-traffic site can experience all kinds of problems, from bored hackers with nothing better to do than ruin your day, to server overload due to a big promotion or major media coverage driving massive amounts of traffic to your site. (What a great problem to have, right?) As your site traffic increases, you may eventually need to move to a private server (Stephanie and Karl both utilize private servers). This is done through your website host and costs more than simply hosting a single site, but it's essential when your site is busy.

This is something you probably won't need to do until your site has been online for a while, but it's important to understand your options for the future of your author-business. For most new authors, a standard website hosting plan that costs between $7 and $20 per month is just fine.

 PRO TIP: Monitor website traffic.

Install Google Analytics on your website. This free tool allows you to monitor your traffic, including how website visitors found your site. It will show you the most commonly used keywords, which pages or blog posts on your site are most popular, what sites link to your site, and much more. We consider this tool essential for all websites: analytics.google.com.

ECOMMERCE

There are countless options for online shopping cart solutions to handle sales on your website. They vary from free to ridiculously expensive. They also vary from single-product versions to something that will run a major department store online. And, finally, they vary from point-and-click to extremely complicated. If you plan to sell your book from your site, along with any additional products, you'll need an ecommerce solution.

If you're selling just one physical product—your book—the easiest option to get started is PayPal. With a standard PayPal account, you can create shopping cart buttons and process payments online. PayPal deposits those fees into your account immediately and allows you to calculate sales tax and collect a fee for shipping.

If you plan to sell multiple products, especially digital products (like downloadable reports), you'll need a more sophisticated shopping cart solution. For digital products in particular, PayPal lacks the functionality needed to handle those transactions. When you sell an electronic report or other digital download, the shopping cart provider should process the payment and then deliver a link to the download that *expires*. You don't want links to your products floating around in the world for all eternity. Download links should expire within a few days of delivery.

Shopping cart solutions offer a variety of features and price points. A savvy virtual assistant or website designer should be able to help you set yours up. Here are some options:

- e-junkie.com (Stephanie's choice)

- volusion.com (Karl's choice)

- 1shoppingcart.com

- payloadz.com

- infusionsoft.com

- woocommerce.com

MERCHANT SERVICES, AKA: *Credit Card Processing*

Traditionally, "merchant services" is the name given to the collection of financial services used by businesses to accept payments via credit cards and ACH (direct transfer). In addition to credit cards, modern merchant services include electronic payment processors such as PayPal.

If you want to accept credit cards at events, you'll need a merchant services account and the ability to swipe credit cards. This process used to be somewhat complicated and expensive, but technology has evolved and it's easier than ever to get a merchant services account.

Credit card processing isn't free and every single entity involved in the sale of your book will take a transaction fee. Some of them charge a monthly or annual fee. Some charge a small transaction fee ($.25 or $.30). All will take a percentage of the sales price. All totaled, it can cost anywhere from $.25 to $1.50 to sell a book.

Keep this in mind when evaluating options for credit card processing. Here are some choices:

Square – This service provides you with a credit card swiper device that plugs into your smartphone or tablet and makes processing mobile sales incredibly easy. You can also use their online service to schedule client appointments or send digital invoices to buyers. If you sell bulk book orders, for example, digital invoices can be handy. Visit Squareup.com.

PayPal – You can get PayPal's mobile payment processing device by requesting it through your account. PayPal also allows you to send digital invoices to buyers and process transactions manually. Visit Paypal.com.

Your Local Bank – All major banks offer merchant card processing services. Whether or not the ease of use and rates are competitive varies greatly so do your homework when considering this option.

PRO TIP: *Take credit cards whether you want to or not.*

Sometimes new authors don't want to take credit cards because they don't want to pay merchant fees or they think it's too complicated. Do yourself a favor and don't fight it. Just take credit cards. Yes, it costs money. But wouldn't you rather have 97% of something than 100% of nothing? You will miss out on sales if you don't accept credit cards.

HOW TO HANDLE SHIPPING FOR YOUR BOOKS

Shipping books is not something authors typically think about until their book is about to be released, but selling books directly is most profitable because you don't have to give up 40% to 55% to retailers. If you want to sell books or other products directly from your website, you'll need to develop a process to ship them.

There are several ways to handle shipping.

- **Media Mail** – The U.S. Postal Service offers media mail, which is a low-cost rate that can be used only for mailing books or other media (like DVDs). You will need to purchase your own envelopes to use media mail (padded envelopes are recommended) and will either have to visit the post office to have your postage printed (a giant pain!) or subscribe to a postage printing service. Good options include Stamps.com or PitneyBowes.com.

    Note that media mail is a fourth-class rate, which means that it takes longer for these packages to arrive at their destination. If you use this service, we recommend paying a few extra cents for tracking so you can find out where a wayward package is located. You also risk packages taking a week or longer to arrive, which can frustrate buyers.

- **Priority Mail** – The U.S. Postal Service makes it easy to use this service by providing free envelopes which you can order from the site (store.usps.com). You can also print postage directly from the USPS website, and even request mail pick-up from a postal carrier at no charge. Priority mail costs a couple of dollars more than media mail, but will arrive much faster and look more professional.

- **Priority Mail Flat Rate** – Flat rate envelopes are also available from the post office and can often save in postage costs, especially when shipping small quantities of books.

- **Federal Express and UPS** – The rates for these services are typically rather high for individual book delivery, but can be competitive when shipping larger quantities of books. It's a good idea to get rate quotes from each, plus the USPS, when shipping one or more cases of books.

Additional Considerations When Shipping Books

- Online buyers expect to pay for shipping. Shipping fees should be passed on to the buyer and incorporated into your ecommerce shopping cart system.

- A postage scale is essential if you want to avoid time-consuming trips to the post office. You can purchase a decent one through an office supply store or online retailer for around $20.

- Readers love an autographed copy, and that can be an incentive to inspire them to buy direct from the author. Take time to personally inscribe and autograph each book—and let buyers know about this on your book sales page.

- Insert marketing collateral into every package. You might include bookmarks, postcards, flyers or materials that promote your other books, services, products, courses, etc.

- You can purchase padded mailers in bulk through shipping stores or online retailers like uline.com. Remember, if you ship first class via USPS, you can use their free envelopes and shipping boxes.

What to do if you don't want to ship books.

It's perfectly acceptable to avoid shipping your own books, but you do need to provide a way for potential readers to purchase. Make it easy for them by including one or more links from your website to an online retailer such as Amazon. While you won't earn as much money on books sold through retailers, routing sales to Amazon can have some perks since you can boost your book's overall sales rank on the site.

You can and should sign up for Amazon's affiliate program, known as Amazon Associates, and earn a small percentage of each book sale generated. With this program, you can generate a link to your book that is embedded with your affiliate code so that when a user clicks through from your website and makes a purchase, you earn a small (itty-bitty, teeny-weeny) percentage of the sale. And, if at the time of purchase the buyer also has other items in her shopping cart, you'll earn a percentage of those items too. You never know. Your book buyer might also decide to buy a kitchen table or a flat-screen TV at the same time as ordering your book! Sign up for the Amazon Associates program here: affiliate-program.amazon.com.

By the way, you can offer your readers a multitude of purchase options. You can allow them to purchase direct from you and/or include links to your favorite indie bookstore, Amazon, BarnesandNoble.com, Smashwords.com, and Audible.com.

"You don't have to be great to start, but you have to start to be great."

—Zig Ziglar

CHAPTER 17
PLAN YOUR BOOK LAUNCH

When preparing to release your book, there are many tasks to be completed. The following list can help you get organized and prepare to make a big splash. But first, some considerations for you before you begin.

DECIDE ON A LAUNCH STRATEGY

You can simply ask people to buy your book or you can offer some added incentive, which can help boost sales. For example, you can compile some bonus items for buyers who register their purchase receipt number (you'll need to create a registration form on your website). Bonuses could include reports, whitepapers, digital workbooks, audio recordings, training videos, checklists, templates, printable coloring pages, or any other downloadable content. This can be content you've created or you can ask peers to contribute bonus items. Bonus downloads can be a wildly popular way to boost book launch results.

Whatever you decide, it's important to plan out your launch strategy in advance. One of the biggest mistakes new authors make is to not think about book marketing until after the book is released.

Also keep in mind that book marketing is a marathon. Authors who see the best results are the ones who commit to ongoing effort and keep those marketing wheels turning. You can do this!

 PRO TIP: *Keep track of your plans.*

Create a file for keeping track of your launch plans. A simple spreadsheet should do the trick. If you're working with a virtual assistant or marketing coach, save your document in a Dropbox.com folder for easy sharing.

WANT TO SELL BOOKS? THE WORK IS JUST BEGINNING.

Before you read on, we want to caution you that the following Book Launch Checklist may overwhelm you. In fact, this entire book probably feels overwhelming, and if it does, please know that you are not alone. The world of book publishing is more complex than most people realize until they dip a toe in and discover that it's more like an ocean than a pond.

It takes a good amount of effort to publish books. You may be thinking the hard part is over, but it's really just beginning. Just because a book is available for sale on Amazon doesn't mean it will sell. There are millions of competing titles. Like it or not, you have to build your tribe and help them find your book.

The following list should help you build a successful book launch. And while the list may seem daunting, know that you don't have to tackle all the tasks. The point is that there is work to be done if you want to sell the books you've worked so hard to write and publish. It's up to you to decide just how much—or how little—work you want to do to drive sales.

If your goal is simply to leave a legacy, entertain your family, or occasionally mail copies of your book to potential clients, then you can probably skip most of the items in this checklist. But if you want to build your platform and generate sales, you'll need to tackle as many of these tasks as possible, either on your own or with the help of a virtual author's assistant.

BOOK LAUNCH CHECKLIST

✓ **Consider hosting a pre-sale (optional).** Making your book available for pre-sale allows you to build some momentum before the book is officially released. Not only can you generate some buzz, but all the pre-sales you accumulate will count toward your total sales ranking on launch day.

✓ **Consider utilizing beta readers (optional).** Beta readers can be a group of 10 to 100 or more people who get early access to read your book for free. Yes, *free.* The goal is to get people talking about your book as soon as it's launched, while you build a base of raving fans and generate reviews. Beta readers can be organized in a private Facebook group and given special privileges, like access to a course you offer to thank them for their efforts. They should also be asked to post book reviews on Amazon, Goodreads, and other sites and encouraged to help you spread the word.

✓ **Plan your launch announcements to happen at least a week AFTER the book is available online.** It can help to give yourself some cushion in your timeline and make sure all sales channels are working properly before you pull the trigger and announce to your audience.

✓ **Build your launch team.** Your launch team should include the people who will help you make your book a success by spreading the word. Your team may include any or all of the following:

- Beta readers
- Friends and family, including current and past coworkers, schoolmates, etc.
- Peers and industry friends
- Fellow authors
- Everyone from your mailing list
- Current and past clients
- Association and nonprofit leaders and members
- Online group leaders and members
- Social media followers

✓ **Build lists of influencers.** Start keeping a list of important people to contact about your book. You can create several lists for different purposes. Your lists can include different groups of people:

- Authors who could provide potential endorsements.
- Members of your launch team.
- Those who will receive review copies: influential people, potential clients, media pros, bloggers, reviewers, etc.
- Trade associations, Meetup groups, alumni groups, and related groups where you can potentially get support for your book.
- Local and national media contacts, online and offline, including radio shows, podcasts, print publications, television, etc.
- Potential bulk buyers such as past clients, corporations, associations, schools, and others who might purchase larger quantities of your books.

- Any person or company that you recommend as a resource in your book. You'll want to notify them, and perhaps they will show their thanks by spreading the word about your book.

- Anyone who contributed to your book in some way. Be sure to send a copy with a note of thanks.

✓ **Create anticipation for your launch.**

- Put your book cover on your website with a big "coming soon" announcement. This can be done months in advance.

- Build your mailing list. Make sure you have an email sign-up box on your website, and add it to your Facebook page as well. Don't have an email list yet? We both use ConstantContact.com. Other options include mailchimp. com and aweber.com.

- Get your social media accounts set up if you don't have them already. You don't need to do it all, but we recommend that you pick at least two of the top networks: Twitter, Facebook, YouTube, LinkedIn, Pinterest or Instagram. Start sharing news about your book months in advance, plus links to all that content you're creating on your new magazine-style website.

✓ **Do pre-launch research.** (Or delegate these tasks to an assistant.):

- Build a media list or purchase a list from a resource such as GebbiePress.com (note that members of the Nonfiction Authors Association receive a discount off Gebbie Press products). Your media list should begin with local print, radio, and television since local media attention is always the easiest to get. Then expand your list to include media outlets across the country.

- Build a list of trade association opportunities. What associations do your potential readers belong to? Visit association websites and look for opportunities. Can you contribute posts to their blog, write for their newsletter or magazine, apply to speak at local meetings or a national event, or even join their board of directors?

- Research bloggers to pitch. Find blogs that reach your target audience and look to see if they post book reviews, accept guest blog posts, conduct interviews or host book giveaway contests.

- Research internet radio shows and podcasts to find programs where you should be a guest. Look for their guest submission guidelines (most need guests).

- Generate book reviews using the strategies we recommended in Chapter 14.

- Look for groups that reach your target audience on Facebook, LinkedIn, Yahoo, and Ning.com. Join one or more groups and start engaging well in advance of your launch so that you aren't a total stranger when it's time to announce your book. Then when it's time to launch your book, you can potentially have hundreds or even thousands of ideal readers interested.

✓ **Write copy to be used for all aspects of the launch.**

- Write and schedule several blog posts to publish during your launch campaign.

- Write and schedule social media posts to publish during your launch campaign. (Use Hootsuite.com to schedule posts.)

- Write an announcement for the online groups you belong to.

- Write email copy and sample social media posts for your launch team to share. (This makes it as easy as possible for them to do so.)

- Write copy you will use to announce to your own email list.

- Write compelling book jacket copy (to be used on your website and other promotional opportunities).

- Write a new author bio with details about your book.

- Write guest blog posts that you will contribute to other websites.

✓ **Write several pitches.**

- Write a pitch for traditional media. Find an angle that isn't just about your book launch (such as a tie-in with an upcoming holiday or recently released statistics).

- Write a pitch for bloggers to review your book, interview you, accept a guest post from you, or host a contest with copies of your book as prizes.

- Write a pitch for podcasters and internet radio shows, pitching yourself as a potential guest.

- Write a pitch for book reviewers.

- Write a pitch for trade association opportunities (contribute to their blogs, newsletters, and magazines, speak at events, get listed in their bookstore, etc.).

✓ **Prep your website.**

- Create a killer book sales page on your website. Make sure to include links to purchase your book on Amazon and other booksellers.

- Add a media page that includes your bio, one or more professional photos, your contact information, and a list of any previous media coverage you've received (or start building that list now). A media page makes it easy for reporters, editors, and producers to learn about you and gather information. Plus, having one on your site will make you look like a pro.

- Add your book announcement on your home page, with a link to your book sales page.

- If you're interested in speaking, add a speaker page to your site with a list of topics you cover, testimonials from previous engagements, and video clips (if available).

✓ **Send pre-launch media pitches.** (Typically up to three months ahead of launch):

- Send out traditional media pitches (print, radio, television). Note that magazines plan their content up to six months in advance.

- Send out blogger pitches.

- Send out internet radio and podcast pitches.

- Note that you can send multiple media pitches over a period of time. Find new angles for your pitches if you don't get a response the first time around. Persistence can pay off!

✓ **Plan a party (if you want one).** Make sure to include a table where you can sign books and be prepared to process credit card payments.

✓ **Set up an Amazon Author Central account.** Claim your book as soon as it is available on AuthorCentral.Amazon.com.

- Update the description for your book and author details.

✓ **Send launch day announcements.**

- Send an email announcement to your mailing list on launch day, and then again throughout the duration of your campaign.

- Send email to peers and clients announcing the launch and asking for support.

- Send email to family and friends announcing the launch.

- Share social media posts on launch day and beyond.

- Send announcement to beta readers, if you have them.

- Announce via social media groups that reach your target audience. (You may need to get permission from the group leader first.)

✓ **Monitor your sales rank on Amazon during launch day.** The lower the rank, the more books you are selling.

✓ **Go live on launch day.** Utilize Facebook Live to engage your audience, report on happenings for the day, and thank your audience.

✓ **Interact with your audience via social media and blog comments throughout your launch period.** Make sure they know you are engaged and grateful for their support.

✓ **Generate book reviews.** Make this a high priority and an *ongoing* task to keep book reviews coming in since these can have a big impact on Amazon sales.

✓ **Additional tasks to consider.**

- Participate in a Goodreads giveaway promotion. LibraryThing also offers similar promotions.

- Apply to participate in a promotion via BookBub.com, which can promote the ebook version of your book at a discount to thousands of readers. This can be a great strategy a few weeks or months after your launch in order to keep the sales momentum going.

- Utilize Amazon Ads to promote your book.

- Think outside the box. What other connections do you have that could help you promote books? Do you belong to an alumni association? Do you serve on the board for a nonprofit? Where can you expand your reach?

- Submit your book to awards programs, which can improve credibility and give you something exciting to promote to your audience. The Nonfiction Authors Association hosts a year-round book awards program: nonfictionauthorsassociation.com/nonfiction-book-awards.

- Host your own free webinars to teleseminars. These should be educational in nature (not just about your book). You can build your mailing list and audience by hosting events like these and requiring attendees to register with an email address.

- Launch your own podcast. Podcasting is hotter than ever and cars are now coming off the assembly line with the podcast app built right into the dashboard! It's easy to start your own show and distribute to iTunes with a tool like Liberated Syndication: libsyn.com.

✓ **Don't forget to have fun!** Marketing a book may not be an easy task, but if you can find a way to enjoy the process, it can go a long way in helping you sell more books and reach more people.

TRACK YOUR BOOK LAUNCH AND MARKETING TASKS

To begin forming your book marketing plan, start by building a list of tasks you plan to execute. We call this a Book Marketing Action Plan, and you can download a free Excel template to build your plan here: nonfictionauthorsassociation.com/reader-bonus.

ADDITIONAL BOOK MARKETING RESOURCES

There are entire books written on book marketing. In fact, Stephanie wrote one: *The Nonfiction Book Marketing Plan: Online and Offline Promotion Strategies to Build Your Audience and Sell More Books.*

We also put together a 20+ page bonus report for you called "Book Marketing Essentials." You can download a free copy here: nonfictionauthorsassociation.com/reader-bonus.

"I've missed more than 9,000 shots in my career. I've lost almost 300 games. Twenty-six times, I've been trusted to take the game winning shot and missed. I've failed over and over and over again in my life. And that is why I succeed."

—Michael Jordan

 **AUTHOR INTERVIEW**

Name: Charmaine Hammond

Book Titles:
Bounce Forward
GPS Your Best Life
On Toby's Terms

Websites: gpsyourbestlife.com and charmainehammond.com

Can you tell us about your publishing journey and why you chose to self-publish your book?

My first published work was in *Chicken Soup for the Soul: What I Learned From the Dog.* I was approached by a publisher who later published my book *On Toby's Terms.* I chose to publish a co-authored book, *GPS Your Best Life,* with that same publisher who then also published my two children's books. I also self-published a book called *Bounce Forward.* I chose to self-publish it and my next two books because it allowed me more flexibility to make the changes I wanted to the book and to create subsidiary products related to the book.

What kind of business are you in and how has your book helped to grow your business?

I have two businesses, one where I speak to corporations on communication, conflict resolution, and collaboration. The book *Bounce Forward*, and my upcoming book *Working Better Together* (both self-published), are used to support my corporate presentations, and for bulk sales to corporations. Both are also credibility products and help generate leads for speaking engagements. (I send them to HR professionals and event planners.)

My second business, co-owned with Rebecca Kirstein, is called Raise a Dream. We teach authors, speakers, and entrepreneurs how to raise their dreams and launch their projects through collaboration. The books we are writing through this brand will be used as a resource for our students and as a lead generator.

What have been some book marketing strategies that have generated the best results for you?

- Selling my books in bulk
- Increasing my speaking fee to include bulk quantities of books with the contract
- Book and speaking tour
- Launch campaigns
- Securing sponsorship to support my book launch and book-related events
- Virtual blog and books tours timed with my launches

Is there anything you would do differently for your next book? Any hard lessons learned?

- Build a marketing plan that has daily activities to sell the book.
- Promote the book in different ways consistently through social media.

- With media find ways to bring people to your website (instead of Amazon) to buy your book or offer a free gift such as a sampler of the book.

- Create systems and processes for the book-related marketing activities that you do on a regular basis.

What advice would you offer to new authors?

- Start planning your marketing while you are still writing the book, otherwise you lose valuable time. While you write you can build your author platform and book media opportunities in advance to coincide with your launch efforts.

- Look for ways to sell your books in bulk as it takes almost as much time to sell them one at a time.

- Explore innovative places to sell your books.

- When you do book signings, do a BOGO offer (Buy One/Get One). Invite people to buy two books, one they keep for themselves and the second to put in a basket to donate to a charity that you have chosen to support.

"It had long since come to my attention that people of accomplishment rarely sat back and let things happen to them. They went out and happened to things."
—Leonardo da Vinci

CHAPTER 18
AUTHOR-PUBLISHER BUSINESS OPERATIONS

B y now, we hope that you understand that by self-publishing, you've gone into business for yourself (if you weren't already in business). You are an entrepreneur, and that means that you also need to think and act like a business owner. This involves managing cash flow, collecting sales tax, managing bookkeeping, and filing business taxes. But it doesn't have to be as daunting as it sounds, and there can be many advantages to business ownership.

BUDGET AND CASH FLOW PROJECTION

It's one thing to create a budget. It's another to create a *realistic* budget that will work for your book project and your business moving forward. Most of the problems in budgets come from optimism. Authors tend to assume they'll sell 500 copies the first week or that every review copy sent out will result in ten immediate sales.

If you put your budget into a nice Excel spreadsheet, you can have a column for each month (January, February, March, etc.). That way you can see how projected sales and other income compares to expenses.

To be effective, you need to be really honest with yourself. Sales numbers come from sales reports. All the expenses related to your business need to be allocated properly. For example, if you drove two hours to deliver a speech, you need to track that mileage.

Sample Budget

Income (January)

Online Book Sales	$1,000
On-site Book Sales	$500
Consulting	$750
Speaking	$1,500
Total Income	$3,750

Expenses

Website	$20
Store Fees	$20
Travel	$320
Printing	$600
Meals	$50
Advertising	$150
Postage	$75
Total Expenses	$1,235

Profit (Income minus Expenses) $2,515

Of course, once you track and report income and expenses, Uncle Sam will view it as a business. The good news is that you may be able to take some nice tax deductions for expenses toward book production, marketing, editors, freelance designers, and even educational materials and memberships you've purchased to help you along the way. Ask your tax pro what you can and can't do.

You might also put headers above each month that say "Projected." Then, when you are done settling accounts for the month, you can change that to "Historic." That will give you a realistic comparison between what you think will happen and reality.

We don't encourage you to revise your projected sales and expenses too often. After all, if you change your projections every time you make a sale, it's really not much of a projection at all. But every quarter (January, April, July, and October) you can adjust your projections and set profit goals. You also need expenses to be realistic. For example, when you start out you won't have any real idea about the cost of shipping. That will become clearer over time.

After a few months you'll have a sense of whether you're making money, and how much. In general, if you're going to be in the book business, you need to take care of the *business* side. A budget with cash-flow projections goes a long way in this regard.

Download a free Cash Flow Forecast Template here: nonfictionauthorsassociation.com/reader-bonus.

LEGAL CONCERNS

First, let's remind you that we are not attorneys or accountants. For qualified legal advice, we recommend hiring an attorney who specializes in publishing law. With that said, we'll share some advice from our own personal experience.

If you are just "you," then publishing is a little easier. As soon as you decide to be in business and you apply for a business license from your local issuing agency, you are automatically operating as a sole proprietor. This means that your business is separate from you as an individual (you should set up a business bank account). And though there are some tax benefits to business ownership, there is little legal protection when you're a sole proprietor.

If you have other business interests or your business life is complicated in any way, then you might consider creating a legal entity for your author-publisher business. This could be an S corporation, LLC, or some other option.

There are two reasons to spend a little time on this. First, if you personally have an estate of any kind that needs to be protected, then an LLC, S-Corp, or some other business entity can separate and protect your personal assets (like your home and retirement accounts) from your business venture. Second, if your publishing activities turn into a nice, big, profitable business, then incorporating can also make sense since it can impact how much you pay in income taxes.

Talk to a professional—Enrolled Agent, CPA or business attorney—about whether, and when, you might want to incorporate.

Warnings and Notices

Every book should have a disclaimer on the copyright page that limits the liability of the author and publisher. Depending on the kind of advice and information you offer in your books, you may need to be more specific about your disclaimer. For example, if you author a health book with medical advice, you need to alert readers that your book should not be a substitute for medical advice and they should consult with their doctor before changing any health regimen.

Fortunately, most people have common sense. The only people who are really a potential problem are the very tiny group that takes your advice verbatim, implements it, somehow manages to mess up their business or their life in some way, AND gets an attorney to agree to blame it on you. This is a highly unusual scenario, but unfortunately, we live in a litigious society.

Most books feature a disclaimer paragraph on the copyright page, and sometimes a further disclaimer in the main text since you can't take chances with things like medical advice. Look at other books in your field to see the kinds of legal statements and liability warnings they include, especially from books produced by the big New York publishers.

Bottom line: Take this stuff seriously, but don't lose sleep over it. Put together a good paragraph, have it reviewed by an attorney, and move on.

SALES TAX

Because you'll be selling a product, you may have to deal with sales tax. Every state is different. For states without sales tax, there may be another permit required to sell products.

And as a reminder, we are not tax professionals or accountants. Please consult a professional to understand how taxes apply for your own unique situation. The following is based on our personal experience with sales tax reporting.

If your state has sales tax, you are probably in for a surprise with regard to how complicated the government can make things. In most states there are multiple layers of tax. There's a state component and a county component. In some areas there's a school district component, a city component, and then special districts. There are special districts for roads, mass transit, libraries, water districts, and pretty much anything you can think of.

For example, in California, there are over 100 different combinations of sales taxes. It all adds up to somewhere between 7% and 9%. As resellers, we are supposed to keep track of sales in every single district. Yes, really.

In addition, when traveling to other states and physically selling books at events, you are supposed to collect and report sales tax for the county where you make sales. It can be incredibly complicated, and the truth is that not everyone follows this rule. It's far easier for big retailers to comply than it is for individuals and small business owners.

In California, depending on the size of your business, sales tax reporting may be required annually (for smaller businesses) and monthly (larger retailers). The report asks you to list the volume of products you purchased at wholesale (without paying sales tax), how many you sold, and at what tax rate. You then remit the report along with payment for sales tax collected.

Since we are based in California, when we make sales over the internet inside of California, we need to collect sales tax. But if we make sales to other states, sales tax collection is not currently required (though this may change soon). Note that if your books are being distributed and sold through Amazon or other retailers, they handle collecting and reporting sales tax for those sales.

If you plan to sell books at events or out of the trunk of your car, you should contact your local government office to apply for a resale license. The IRS provides a list of agencies for all states here: irs.com/articles/state-sales-taxes.

By the way, your resale license also gives you the ability to purchase your books (and other products intended for resale) at wholesale, meaning you will not pay sales tax when you purchase your books from your printer. However, you must still collect, report, and pay sales tax each time you sell a copy or keep one for personal use.

Please don't let sales tax collection scare you. Though it sounds complicated, if you keep simple records of your transactions, it doesn't have to be too painful.

BUSINESS LICENSE

If you want to take your business seriously, you should apply for a business license. Licenses are typically issued in the county where your business is located and the fee is nominal—usually around $100 per year. Your state may also require an additional license.

In addition to the business license, you will need to file a DBA—Doing Business As. This is the name you assign to your business. It could be your publishing company name or something broader. Karl operates Great Little Book Publishing Co., Inc. as an S-Corp with DBA for Small Biz Thoughts. Stephanie operates Stephanie Chandler Enterprises, LLC with separate DBAs for Authority Publishing and the Nonfiction Authors Association.

The DBA gives you the ability to set up a business bank account, which is *absolutely essential*. The IRS requires that business and personal expenses be maintained separately so your business bank account will keep you from getting into some potential hot water down the road. If you deposit funds from book sales into your personal checking account, you risk the IRS hammer coming down on you—and that's no fun at all.

EMPLOYER IDENTIFICATION NUMBER

An Employer Identification Number (EIN) is a 9-digit identifier issued by the IRS to business entities operating in the United States. This allows you to use the assigned number on business tax forms instead of your Social Security number. If you offer freelance services of any kind or you're required to issue W-9 forms to other businesses each year, having an EIN prevents you from having to share your social security number.

It's easy to apply for an EIN and it's completely free. You can learn more and apply for yours here: irs.gov/businesses/small-businesses-self-employed/employer-id-numbers.

BUSINESS INSURANCE

Many authors don't even think about business insurance, but if your books offer advice on health, finances, or other potentially risky topics, you may want to consider acquiring some inexpensive general liability insurance. Some providers to consider: TheHartford.com and hiscox.com/small-business-insurance.

HIRING HELP

Stephanie has had a personal motto for several years: "The more people I hire, the more money I earn." One of the best ways to grow your author business is to hire the right people to help free up your time so that you can focus on what you do best. While you may think you can't afford to hire help, consider how outsourcing certain tasks can actually help you earn more money.

For example, if you can hire someone for $20 per hour to do administrative tasks, bookkeeping, or graphic design, and you earn $50 or more per hour by consulting or speaking, then you come out ahead. When you reclaim an hour of your own time, you can use that hour to generate revenue, instead of handling tasks you don't like (such as bookkeeping—blech!).

One of the great benefits of doing business in the digital age is that you don't necessarily have to hire employees unless you're ready to do so. There are all kinds of freelancers available to handle tasks for you on an as-needed basis, which eliminates the need for worker's comp insurance and managing payroll.

Of course, the government has strict guidelines around hiring freelancers. In several states, including California, companies that hire contractors must be able to answer "The ABC Test:"

A. The contractor provides services free from the company's control. (For example, sets his/her own work hours.)

B. Service provided must be a task that is outside of the company's core business. (For example, the freelance designer you hire to create your book cover.)

C. Contractor is engaged in providing services to other clients.

Freelancers are independent contractors who are responsible for their own business licensing, banking, and taxes. When you hire a freelancer, you must send a 1099 tax form at the end of the year, detailing how much was paid. Again, a tax planner can handle this for you, and it doesn't have to be as complicated as it sounds. This also means you should ask for a W-9 form from any freelancer you hire, and you can find blank forms via the IRS website at no charge. A W-9 provides you with the freelancer's contact information and tax ID so you can issue that 1099 at the end of the year.

In addition, you should have a standard work-for-hire agreement with any freelancer that you hire. This should detail their status as an independent contractor. You can find contracts online or via nolo.com.

HIRE A VIRTUAL ASSISTANT

Book marketing can be an incredibly time-consuming task, leaving many authors feeling frustrated and overwhelmed. After all, few authors have the luxury of writing and promoting books full time. Most of us, and even *New York Times* bestselling authors, have day jobs, families, and life commitments.

We firmly believe that every serious author needs to hire an assistant, and the easiest way to do so is to hire a virtual assistant (VA). Virtual assistants typically work from their own homes and you can retain their services for as few as five hours per month. The right assistant can take over the tasks you don't have time to handle, as well as the tasks you don't enjoy, freeing you up to focus on writing your next book, building your business, or attending your kids' Little League games!

Assistants have all kinds of experience levels and their rates can vary greatly depending on their level of experience. Most work on an hourly basis and offer packages of retainer hours each month. This means you can hire someone for just a few hours per month or ramp things up and hire for 10+ hours per week if your budget allows.

Plan to spend $20 to $100 per hour, depending on the experience level. And while that may sound like a substantial investment, keep in mind that these are independent contractors who pay their own business taxes and expenses. And when you hire a contractor, you avoid the expense of workers comp insurance and payroll.

Also, spending a few hundred dollars per month on administrative assistance can be a game-changer for your author career. If hiring someone else frees up your time to secure speaking engagements, consulting gigs, or other high-dollar business, or they help you land those paid opportunities, then having a virtual assistant will pay for itself many times over.

WHERE TO HIRE ASSISTANTS, GRAPHIC DESIGNERS, AND OTHER FREELANCERS

There are a number of resources where you can submit a Request for Proposal (RFP) or post a job description and receive information from applicants.

- **Authors Assistants** – A directory of virtual assistants who have completed training programs to specifically support authors: instructionsmith.com/professional-virtual-authors-assistants.

- **IVAA** – The International Virtual Assistants Association offers a member directory, plus an option to post a Request for Proposal (RFP): ivaa.org.

- **AssistU** – A training program for virtual assistants where you can find assistants who have been through certification programs: assistu.com.

- **Upwork** – This is the largest network for finding all kinds of freelance professionals in many countries. Options include web designers, copywriters, graphic designers, administrative professionals, and much more. Because Upwork manages the hiring and payment process for you, one big benefit is that you won't have to collect W-9 forms or issue 1099s to those hired through this site: Upwork.com.

- **Fiverr** – This service lists people and the tasks they are willing to complete for $5. It can be handy for quick tasks like getting banner ads and social media headers designed: fiverr.com.

- **Guru** – Similar to Upwork, find freelance professionals: guru.com.

- **Freelancer** – Similar to Upwork and Guru: freelancer.com.

- **Craigslist** – If you prefer to work with someone local, you can always advertise job opportunities with Craigslist—even for contractor positions: craigslist.org.

- **99 Designs** – This is a fun way to find a graphic designer. It's done by conducting a contest and allowing designers to contribute their concepts. Pick the one you like best and you can award the fee to the winning designer: 99designs.com.

- **Envato** – Directory of freelance graphic designers: envato.com.

- **Interns** – Guess what? Students can work for free or at a low cost. They want to learn and gain experience and you can create a mutually beneficial situation by teaching someone what you do while they help manage tasks. Contact your local colleges to inquire about placing an ad for an intern. There will be some paperwork involved, but this can be a great solution that can also lead to a potential employee for your business. Do note that some states *require* that you pay interns and also have specific guidelines you must follow (like making it an educational experience for the intern) so check the guidelines for your state first.

- **Nonfiction Authors Association Recommended Resources** – We maintain a list of resources, including freelancers who specialize in editing, book production, and more: nonfictionauthorsassociation.com/recommended-resources.

AUTHOR BUSINESS STARTUP CHECKLIST

Use this checklist to get your business in order, and don't forget to run it all by a qualified attorney and tax professional.

Business Licensing

✓ Choose a business name or publishing company name or both

✓ File for business license (county)

✓ File a DBA (Doing Business As)

✓ File for an EIN (Employer Identification Number)

✓ File for a resale license (sales tax, county)

✓ File a trademark for your business name or signature process (optional)

Financials

✓ Open a business bank account

✓ Keep all receipts

✓ Start proper bookkeeping practices (hire out or do yourself)

✓ Hire a tax planner or accountant

✓ Create a cash-flow forecast

✓ Establish a budget

Legal

✓ Establish business entity (sole proprietor, LLC or S corporation)

✓ Add a website disclaimer and privacy policy

✓ Acquire liability insurance

Logistics

✓ Set up your office (home or outside)

✓ Get a post office box

✓ Acquire shipping supplies

✓ Purchase a postage scale

Hiring Considerations

✓ Virtual assistant

✓ Graphic designer

✓ Web designer

✓ Editor

✓ Proofreader

✓ Typesetter

✓ Indexer

✓ Publicist

✓ Marketing firm

✓ Bookkeeper

✓ Attorney

✓ Accountant

Graphic Design

✓ Business logo design

✓ Website design

✓ Business card design

✓ Marketing collateral (flyers, postcards, bookmarks, etc.)

✓ Book cover design

Tools and Software

✓ Toll-free phone line (use a service like Grasshopper.com or RingCentral.com)

✓ Commercial email delivery

✓ Webinar/teleseminar

✓ Photos/images editing

✓ Postage printing

✓ Credit card processing (in-person)

✓ Ecommerce

✓ Skype

✓ Web camera

✓ Contact management

✓ Project management

Enjoying this book?

The best way to thank a fellow author
is to post a review on Amazon!
(Pretty please? Thank you!)

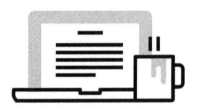

CHAPTER 19
HOW TO GET A TRADITIONAL BOOK DEAL

While this book is focused on self-publishing for nonfiction, many authors wonder about the traditional publishing process and whether or not going this route makes sense. If you're curious about this option, read on.

TRADITIONAL BOOK DEAL CHECKLIST

✓ Develop your platform for book sales. Publishers give priority consideration to authors with a large platform (audience).

✓ Decide on a concept for your book—something unique that will stand out against competition.

✓ Define your target audience to ensure you have a market for the book.

✓ Evaluate the competition to ensure there is market demand and that your book has a unique hook.

✓ Write a query letter to send to agents and/or editors. A query is your initial point of contact.

✓ Write a complete proposal and at least two sample chapters to send to agents/editors upon request.

✓ Research and then contact agents until you find one who is excited about your project—or research smaller publishing houses and contact them directly. Most agents and publishers list submission guidelines on their websites.

✓ Negotiate a contract and sign a deal.

✓ Finish writing your book by the due date outlined in your contract.

✓ Proceed through the editing process, which can take months to complete.

✓ Launch the new book and market the heck out of it.

LITERARY AGENTS

While most small and mid-size publishers accept book proposals directly, the largest publishing houses will only work with literary agents. If you want to receive a substantial book advance and get published with a big press (such as Random House), then you will need to work with an agent.

A literary agent acts as a liaison between an author and a publishing house. Literary agents take a percentage of the book deals that they make, which typically amounts to around 10% of U.S. rights and 15% if they sell foreign rights (the rights for your book to be published in another country). Many agents also charge back to clients for photocopying and shipping. Reputable agents do not charge fees to read a book proposal or manuscript so beware of any agent that requires a fee upfront.

Once an author signs a contract with an agent, the agent then helps the author fine-tune his proposal and prepare it for submission to publishers. When the proposal is ready, the agent then sends it to her publishing contacts and navigates the nego-tiation process and contract terms.

The agent and the author share the same goal: to get the largest book advance possible. An advance is what the publisher pays the author in anticipation of book sales. The publisher estimates how much revenue the book sales will generate and bases the advance on that figure.

Authors don't earn any royalties on book sales until the advance is earned back. Once that happens, royalties are paid to the author based on a percentage agreed to in the author's pub-lishing contract, with rates ranging from 8% to 15% of either the wholesale or retail price of the book. For new authors, a book advance can be as low as $2,500. Some well-known authors receive advances well into the six-figures. Celebrities often receive seven-figure advances.

Advances are typically paid in installments, which are made during the course of the agreement. For example, you may be offered 33% up front, 33% upon submission of your completed manuscript, and the remaining balance when the book goes to press.

When working with an agent, royalties are paid to the agent, and then the agent takes her cut and sends the remaining payment to the author. Royalty payment schedules are typically slow. Most publishers send payments just once or twice per year.

HOW TO FIND AN AGENT

Each agent has a special interest and focuses on books in certain genres. This usually reflects the agent's personal reading tastes and the contacts she has at various publishing houses. It would be a waste of time to send a book proposal for a cookbook to an agent who specializes in children's books, so it's important to research agents and their specialties before wasting anyone's time with an inappropriate pitch.

Authors should keep in mind one important point: *agents need authors as much as authors need agents!* Agents make their living off their authors, and therefore want to work with authors who they believe have the most potential for sales. Part of this equation is dictated by the publishers. Publishers don't like to gamble on new authors unless there is a compelling reason to do so.

Most of the larger publishing houses, and therefore agents, seek authors with a built-in platform. A platform is essentially the author's audience and reflects the author's ability to sell the book. The publisher wants to know that the author has an audience of buyers waiting for the book. A good author platform means that the author has a national presence through speaking engagements, internet exposure, social media, writing a national column, hosting a popular radio show or having some other kind of celebrity status that reaches large numbers of potential readers.

Previous media exposure is also helpful. Has the author been on TV, radio, or in print? Your past experience also counts toward your platform. Publishers and agents don't want to hear what you will start doing after your book is released. (*"I will start blogging! I will start speaking!"*) They want to know how you are reaching your audience today.

Without a platform, it is far more difficult to convince big publishers to take a chance on a new author, though not impossible. Small and mid-sized publishers, however, may still consider a new author if the book idea is convincing enough.

Most agents and smaller publishing houses detail their submission requirements on their websites so that authors know what to send and how it should be delivered. In most cases, agents want to see a query letter first so they can get an idea of what your book is about and whether it's a good fit for them.

Most agencies accept queries via email. A query letter should include a brief synopsis of the book with a solid hook. This is your chance to convince the agent that there is an audience for the book and that you are the person to write about the subject. Include a brief author bio detailing your specific qualifications for writing the book. You don't necessarily have to be an expert on a subject to write about it, but if you're not, you should have statistics and interviews from sources who are.

If the agent is intrigued by your query letter, she will request a book proposal and sample chapters. Be sure you have these items ready to go before you send out query letters.

CONTACT PUBLISHERS DIRECTLY

There are hundreds of small and mid-size publishing houses that may be willing to consider your book without the assistance of an agent. The best way to locate these is to examine books in your genre. Find out who is publishing the books in your subject area and begin researching your options. Most publishers have websites where they detail what they expect from the submission process.

Similar to the query letter that you would write an agent, you can use a query letter to contact smaller publishers directly.

RESOURCES FOR FINDING AGENTS AND PUBLISHERS

- The Association of Authors' Representatives, Inc. is a member-based organization for agents who follow a defined code of conduct: aar-online.org.

- *Guide to Literary Agents* by Chuck Sambuchino.

- Publishers Marketplace offers a directory of agents: publishersmarketplace.com.

- Writer's Market offers a directory of agents: writersmarket.com/cms/open/agent.

- Poets and Writers offers a directory of small publishing houses: pw.org/small_presses.

- Go to the bookstore or library to check out books in your genre. Most authors give a special thanks to their agent or editor in the acknowledgments section.

- If you locate an agent and aren't sure about her reputation, try a Google search. You can also ask for referrals to other authors who have worked with the agent. Remember, the agents need authors as much as you need them. You have every right to do your homework and make sure the agent is a good fit for you.

- Search competing books on Amazon and locate the publishers, then go to each publisher's website and look for submission guidelines. Many small to mid-sized presses accept pitches directly (no agent needed). This is an especially good strategy for authors of books on niche topics.

- Here are guidelines for writing a query letter: writersdigest-shop.com/query-letter.

- Here are examples of successful query letters: adweek.com/galleycat/agent-query-letters-that-actually-worked-for-nonfiction/69941.

ELEMENTS OF A BOOK PROPOSAL

A good book proposal should be convincing, thorough, and fully edited for spelling and grammatical errors. Your proposal reflects you and your professionalism, so make sure it demonstrates your best work and follows industry standards. Proposals can range from 10 to 50 pages. Remember to check the website of the agent or publisher you are pitching to see if they provide specific guidelines for proposals you send to them.

In general, a proposal should have the following elements:

- ✓ Typed on 8.5 x 11 white, standard bond paper.
- ✓ Contents should be double-spaced.
- ✓ A footer should indicate the author's name and book title.
- ✓ Pages numbered consecutively.
- ✓ A standard font, such as Times New Roman, in 12-point size for easy reading.
- ✓ If sending via postal mail, it should not be stapled or bound with anything other than a large binder clip.

The following is an outline you can use to create your book proposal:

Cover Page – This should include the book title, subtitle, author name, estimated word count for the final book (typically 40,000 to 80,000 words, depending on the genre), and author's contact information (address, phone number, email address and website link).

Overview – Two to five pages that highlight the most important elements of the book. Keep in mind that your first few paragraphs are your best chance to hook the agent or editor. If these paragraphs aren't immediately engaging, the rest of your proposal may not be read. Explain why the world needs this book, what the book is about, and why you are the best person to write it. If you're able to obtain any endorsements from celebrities or well-known authors, list them.

Market Analysis – One or two pages that explain who your target readers are. Are you targeting single mothers, people with food allergies, or corporate executives? Baseball fans, dog owners or teenagers? List any recent statistics that support your case for a broad audience.

Competitive Analysis – List at least five books that would compete with your title. Explain the strengths and weaknesses of each and how your book will be different or better. Make sure to cite the author, publisher, and date of publication for each book. If you haven't read your competitors' books, you will need to do so in order to complete this section. It is also a great way to help you structure your book since evaluating the competition is sure to give you some ideas for ways to make your book better.

Promotion Plan – Two or more pages that describe how you will market the book. This is an important element of your proposal so put a lot of thought and substance in this section. List any media experience and contacts that you currently have. If your website receives a lot of traffic, you write a national column, you are a public speaker reaching thousands each year, you have a massive social media following or have any other major audience credentials, list details here.

Keep in mind that most publishers don't spend much money to promote new authors. You can offer to do a book tour but will most likely have to fund the tour yourself. If you have a significant amount of money that you plan to contribute to promotion efforts, indicate this here by saying, "The author is willing to match the publisher's promotion budget up to $xxxx.xx." If you plan to spend less than $5,000, leave this statement out.

Chapter Outline – Include chapter titles and key points for each chapter. This can be a bulleted list or several paragraphs describing each chapter.

Author Bio – Give a brief overview of your qualifications, previous writing credits, and anything that will justify why you are the right person to write this book. This is not the place to list your hobbies, pets, or other irrelevant details. Stick to the topic at hand and demonstrate your authority on the subject. Most importantly, if you have a large following (huge mailing list, regular speaking engagements, etc.), make sure you indicate it here.

Delivery Information – This is a short paragraph that lists the estimated word count of the completed manuscript, and the number of months needed to complete the manuscript.

Sample Chapters – Include one to three sample chapters. If your book is a memoir or other narrative nonfiction, know that the quality of the writing is of the utmost importance. Have your chapters fully edited and ready for prime time prior to sending.

Supporting Documentation – Include copies of published articles, publicity materials, and anything that demonstrates your talents, accomplishments, and promotional abilities.

PUBLISHING CONTRACTS

If a publisher offers you a contract, get ready for your head to spin. These contracts can vary greatly in what they offer and what they expect from the author. In general, a contract will outline the following:

Payment Terms

A book advance fee ranging from $2,500 to $10,000 is most typical for first-time authors without a substantial platform. As mentioned previously, advances are usually paid over time; some pay half at contract signing, and half after the manuscript is accepted (after the final editing process is complete). Some pay in thirds: one third upon contract signing, one third upon acceptance, and one third when the book is published.

Royalty rates are paid after the book earns back the initial advance. Then royalties are paid based on a percentage of the book's retail or, more commonly, wholesale price. Typical percentages are 8% to 15% of the wholesale price, and the percentages may increase on a tiered scale depending on the number of books sold. You will also receive a separate percentage for ebook sales.

The terms for sales of foreign rights, audio or book club rights are typically split 50/50 between the publisher and the author. For example, if the publisher sells the rights to reprint your book in France for $2,000, they will deduct any related expenses and split the remaining balance with you.

Rights

Generally, when you sign a contract with a publisher, you are giving up control over your work. The contract may require that you do not reprint any portion of your manuscript in any other format. You may be allowed to use portions of the text for reprinting in magazines or other promotional venues. The publisher may also request the right to change the title of your book and will have full control over your book's cover design.

The publisher will also specify the amount of time they have in order to publish your book. This timeframe can range from 12 months to three years. Yes, really! If they don't publish within the agreed timeframe, you have the right to cancel your contract.

Remember that you will also be involved in the editing process. Your manuscript will be reviewed by a copy editor and sent to you with requests for revisions. This process can take months and you may go back and forth several times before you receive the final copy for approval.

If you receive a book contract offer directly (without an agent), use due diligence and hire a literary attorney or experienced consultant who can help you review the terms of the contract and understand typical negotiation points. Whenever you sign your name to any legal document, you should be well-informed and know exactly what you're getting into. Determine what criteria are most important to you and don't be afraid to ask for some changes. The publisher may or may not be willing to negotiate, but you won't know unless you ask!

ADDITIONAL RESOURCES

- *How to Write a Book Proposal* by Michael Larsen and Jody Rein
- Nonfiction book proposal outline from Ted Weinstein, literary agent: twliterary.com/bookproposal

The process of pursuing a book deal can provide good industry education for authors. You may receive feedback from agents and editors that helps your book be more successful in the long run. Just know that the process takes time. Locating contacts, doing research, sending queries, and sending proposals can take months or even years. And if you're offered a deal, you will again wait at least another year before your book reaches bookshelves. But if this is an important goal for you, these timelines should be just small obstacles to overcome.

YOU CAN DO THIS!

We want you to know that success with book publishing is entirely possible, and it can be a fun and rewarding journey. Both Stephanie and Karl have enjoyed careers spanning more than a decade. We love the freedom we've created with our respective businesses, and the opportunities we have to make a difference in the lives of our readers and clients each day. You can, too!

We want to challenge you to tackle three tasks each day to move you closer to your goals. That might include writing a few pages in your latest manuscript, recording a video for your YouTube channel, pitching yourself as a guest on a podcast, writing a blog post or reaching out to a potential book reviewer. The fact is that even just a few small tasks done daily can add up to big results over time.

Just three per day! You can do that, right?

We would love for you to join our tribe at the Nonfiction Authors Association. Members receive many benefits, including access to a private member forum where we discuss all kinds of publishing-related topics. Learn more and join us here: NonfictionAuthorsAssociation.com.

WILL YOU HELP US SPREAD THE WORD?

One of the best ways to thank a fellow author is to help raise awareness for his or her book. If you enjoyed this book, we would be grateful if you could help us with any of the following:

- Post a book review on Amazon, Goodreads, BN.com, your blog or another website.

- Tell your friends or anyone you think would enjoy this book.

- Recommend or mention the book in any writing/publishing-related online groups you belong to.

- Loan your copy to someone who needs it.

- Buy copies for all of your writer friends! (And if you have a lot of friends, contact us for a bulk discount rate!)

- Recommend us as speakers for your local writers association conferences and events. We love to travel and can deliver webinars too.

Consider this a deposit in the good karma bank that will hopefully come back around to you! (And make sure you put a request like this in your own book.)

We thank you and wish you much success on your own author journey,

Stephanie and Karl

RESOURCES FOR NONFICTION WRITERS

If you would like to download a printable version of this list, you can do so here: nonfictionauthorsassociation.com/reader-bonus.

ADVERTISING

- Google Adwords: adwords.google.com
- Google Adsense: adsense.google.com
- Facebook: facebook.com/business
- Bing: bingads.microsoft.com
- Oath (For Yahoo!, AOL, MSN, and other sites): oath.com

AFFILIATE SALES

- Clickbank: clickbank.com

- Commission Junction: cj.com
- JV Zoo: jvzoo.com

AMAZON

- Author Central: authorcentral.amazon.com
- Associates (affiliate): affiliate-program.amazon.com
- Advantage (sell books directly): advantage.amazon.com
- Seller Central: sellercentral.amazon.com
- Kindle Direct Publishing: kdp.amazon.com
- Customer Support for Authors: authorcentral.amazon.com/gp/help/contact-us
- Kindle Pay-Per-Click Advertising Overview: kdp.amazon.com/en_US/help/topic/G201499010

BOOK AWARDS

- Nonfiction Book Awards: nonfictionauthorsassociation.com/nonfiction-book-awards
- Ben Franklin Book Awards: ibpabenjaminfranklinawards.com
- Global Ebook Awards: globalebookawards.com
- Foreword Book of the Year: forewordreviews.com/services/book-awards/botya
- Nautilus Book Awards: nautilusbookawards.com
- The Eric Hoffer Awards: hofferaward.com

BOOK CLUBS

- From Left to Write: fromlefttowrite.com
- Book Club Reading List: bookclubreading.com
- Meetup: meetup.com

BOOK MARKETING

- NetGalley (book review service): netgalley.com
- Bookbub (ebook promotions): bookbub.com

BUSINESS RESOURCES

- IRS Sales Tax Permits by State: irs.com/articles/state-sales-taxes
- Business Liability Insurance: TheHartford.com and hiscox. com/small-business-insurance

CONTESTS

- Rafflecopter: rafflecopter.com
- Gleam: gleam.io
- Goodreads Giveaways: goodreads.com/giveaway
- LibraryThing: librarything.com
- BookLikes: booklikes.com

EBOOKS AND AUDIOBOOKS

- Amazon Kindle: KDP.Amazon.com
- Barnes and Noble Nook: NookPress.com

- Apple iBookstore: itunes.com/sellyourbooks
- Kobo Books: writinglife.kobobooks.com
- Google Play: play.google.com/books/publish/
- Smashwords: smashwords.com
- Audiobook Creation Exchange: acx.com
- Findaway Voices: findaway.com/findaway-voices
- Book Funnel (distribute your ebook to beta readers): bookfunnel.com
- Audible (largest ebook retailer): audible.com

EMAIL MARKETING

- Constant Contact: constantcontact.com
- AWeber: aweber.com
- MailChimp: mailchimp.com
- Gmail (we recommend switching to Gmail if you still have AOL, Hotmail, or Yahoo Mail): google.com/gmail

EVENT REGISTRATION MANAGEMENT

- EventBrite: eventbrite.com
- Evite: evite.com
- Meetup: meetup.com

FREELANCERS

- Upwork (formerly Elance): upwork.com
- 99 Designs: 99designs.com

- Fiverr: fiverr.com
- Freelancer: freelancer.com
- Envato: envato.com
- Writers Boon: writersboon.com

GRAPHIC DESIGN

- Canva: canva.com
- Designrr: go.designrr.io
- Fiverr: fiverr.com/
- Upwork: upwork.com
- 99Designs: 99designs.com
- Stock Layouts (pre-designed templates): stocklayouts.com

MARKET RESEARCH

- Trendwatching: Trendwatching.com
- Market Research Reports: marketresearch.com
- Buzzsumo (content trends): app.buzzsumo.com
- Google Trends: trends.google.com
- SCIP (hire researchers): scip.org

ONLINE COURSE TOOLS

- Kajabi: kajabi.com
- Lynda: lynda.com
- Udemy: udemy.com

- Viddler: viddler.com
- Creative Live: creativelive.com
- Teachable: teachable.com

PAYMENT PROCESSING

- PayPal: paypal.com
- Square: squareup.com
- Amazon Payments: pay.amazon.com
- Authorize: authorize.net

PODCASTING

- Liberated Syndication: libsyn.com
- Audacity (recording and editing): audacityteam.org
- Adobe Audition (audio editing): adobe.com/audition
- Pamela for Skype (recording): pamela.biz
- Garage Band (recording for Mac, pre-installed)
- Ecamm (recording for Mac): ecamm.com/mac/callrecorder/
- iTunes: apple.com/itunes/podcasts
- Stitcher (podcast directory for Android phones): stitcher.com/content-providers
- Microphones: Audio Technica, Blue Yeti, Heil, Pop Filter (to filter sound)

PRINTING AND PROMOTIONAL PRODUCTS

- PS Print: PSPrint.com

- Vistaprint: vistaprint.com
- iPrint: iprint.com
- Next Day Flyers: nextdayflyers.com
- 4 Imprint: 4imprint.com
- Affordable Buttons: affordablebuttons.com

PROFESSIONAL SPEAKING

- Prezi (presentation software alternative to PowerPoint): prezi.com
- National Speakers Association (NSA): nsaspeaker.org
- Toastmasters: Toastmasters.org
- Association for Talent Development: td.org
- American Seminar Leaders Association: asla.com
- Speaker Net News (newsletter): SpeakerNetNews.com
- Slideshare: slideshare.net

PUBLICITY

- Help a Reporter: helpareporter.com
- Cision's Media Database (formerly Bacon's): us.cision.com
- Gebbie Press (media databases): gebbiepress.com
- Muck Rack (find media sources on Twitter): muckrack.com
- Newspapers (free directory): newspapers.com
- PR Web (press releases): PRWeb.com
- Profnet Connect (directory of experts): profnetconnect.com

PUBLISHING

- ACES: The Society for Editing: aceseditors.org
- Editorial Freelancers Association: the-efa.org
- Association of Ghostwriters associationofghostwriters.org
- American Society for Professional Indexing: asindexing.org
- My Identifiers (ISBNs and Barcodes): myidentifiers.com
- Canada ISBN registration: bac-lac.gc.ca
- Library of Congress Control Number: loc.gov/publish
- Copyright Office (official, register your manuscript here): copyright.gov
- Fonts for Sale/Download: fontshop.com and myfonts.com

PUBLISHING: BOOK DISTRIBUTORS

- Ingram Content Group, Inc. (world's largest book distributor): IngramContent.com
- Independent Publishers Group (IPG): ipgbook.com
- Baker & Taylor (largest supplier of books to libraries): Baker-Taylor.com
- Publishers Group West (largest distributor of independent titles in the U.S.): pgw.com
- BCH Fulfillment & Distribution (for small presses): Bookch.com
- List of Book Distributors: nonfictionauthorsassociation.com/list-of-book-distributors-and-wholesalers

PUBLISHING: BOOK DISTRIBUTORS—LIBRARY MARKET

- Overdrive: Overdrive.com
- ProQuest: proquest.com
- Bibliotheca: bibliotheca.com

PUBLISHING: BOOK PRINTERS

- IngramSpark: ingramspark.com
- Lightning Source (for publishers with multiple titles): lightningsource.com
- Baker & Taylor Publisher Services: btpubservices.com
- Full List of Book Printers: nonfictionauthorsassociation.com/list-of-book-printers-in-the-united-states-states-international

PUBLISHING: LITERARY AGENTS

- The Association of Authors' Representatives: aar-online.org
- Publishers Marketplace: publishersmarketplace.com
- Writer's Market: writersmarket.com

ROYALTY-FREE IMAGES

- iStock Photo: istockphoto.com
- 123RF: 123rf.com
- Clipart: clipart.com
- Flickr: flickr.com/creativecommons
- Pixabay: pixabay.com

ROYALTY-FREE MUSIC

- Pond 5: pond5.com

- Music Bakery: musicbakery.com

SCREEN CAPTURE

- Snagit: techsmith.com/screen-capture.html

- Screenflow (for Mac): telestream.net/screenflow/

- Camtasia (desktop video recording): techsmith.com/video-editor. html

SHIPPING

- United States Postal Service: usps.com

- Stamps.com (print your own postage): stamps.com

- USPS Postage Calculator: postcalc.usps.com

- Pitney Bowes: pitneybowes.com

- Uline (supplies): uline.com

SHOPPING CARTS

- E-Junkie: e-junkie.com

- 1ShoppingCart: 1shoppingcart.com

- Payloadz: payloadz.com

- Infusionsoft: infusionsoft.com

- Gumroad: gumroad.com

SOCIAL MEDIA TOOLS

- Tweetdeck: tweetdeck.com

- Hootsuite: hootsuite.com

- Buffer: buffer.com

- Pay with a Tweet: paywithatweet.com

- Sponsored Tweets: sponsoredtweets.com

- Bitly (link shortener): bit.ly

SOFTWARE AND TECHNOLOGY TOOLS

- CNET (free software downloads): download.cnet.com/windows/

- Journey Ed (discounted software for students): journeyed.com

- Carbonite (online backup—essential!): carbonite.com

- Dropbox: dropbox.com

- Dragon Naturally Speaking (recording transcription software): nuance.com/dragon

TELESEMINARS AND WEBINARS

- Zoom: Zoom.us

- Go to Meeting: gotomeeting.com

- Google Hangouts: hangouts.google.com

- Stealth Webinar: stealthseminar.com

- Audio Acrobat: audioacrobat.com

- Instant Teleseminar: instantteleseminar.com

- Free Conference: freeconference.com
- Skype Recording: pamela.biz/en

VIDEO SHARING

- YouTube: youtube.com
- Vimeo: vimeo.com
- Periscope: periscope.tv

VIRTUAL ASSISTANTS

- Authors Assistants: instructionsmith.com/professional-virtual-authors-assistants/
- Assist U: assistu.com
- International Virtual Assistants Association: ivaa.org

WEBSITE HOSTING AND DOMAINS

- ServInt: servint.com
- GoDaddy: godaddy.com
- Network Solutions: networksolutions.com
- Blue Host: bluehost.com

WEBSITE TOOLS

- Lead Pages (landing pages): leadpages.net
- Unbounce (landing pages, pop-ups): unbounce.com
- Google Analytics (traffic monitoring): analytics.google.com

- Clicky (real-time site analytics): clicky.com
- Button Factory (create website buttons): dabuttonfactory.com
- W3 Schools (HTML tutorial and tags): w3schools.com/html/default.asp
- Google Keyword Planner: adwords.google.com/home/tools/keyword-planner
- Feedburner (blog feed): feedburner.google.com

WORDPRESS TEMPLATES

- Theme Forest: themeforest.net
- Elegant Themes: elegantthemes.com
- Template Monster: templatemonster.com
- A Themes: athemes.com

WRITING TOOLS

- Citation Machine (locate citations): citationmachine.net
- Pro Writing Aid (editing tool): prowritingaid.com
- Grammarly: grammarly.com
- Thesaurus: thesaurus.com
- Dictionary: dictionary.com

WRITERS' GROUPS AND CONFERENCES

- Nonfiction Authors Association: nonfictionauthorsassociation.com
- Independent Book Publishers Association: ibpa-online.org

- Nonfiction Writers Conference: NonfictionWritersConference.com
- Shaw Guides (list of writers conferences): writing.shawguides.com/
- Publishing University: publishinguniversity.org/
- San Francisco Writers Conference: sfwriters.org
- San Francisco Writing for Change: sfwritingforchange.org

MISCELLANEOUS TOOLS

- Grammarly (spelling & grammar check): grammarly.com
- Gravatar (get your photo posted alongside comments): en.gravatar.com
- Survey Monkey: surveymonkey.com
- Talkwalker (alternative to Google Alerts): talkwalker.com/alerts

Additional resources, including recommended service providers: nonfictionauthorsassociation.com/recommended-resources

ABOUT THE AUTHORS

Stephanie Chandler is the author of several books including:

- *The Nonfiction Book Marketing Plan: Online and Offline Promotion Strategies to Build Your Audience* and *Sell More Books*

- *Own your Niche: Hype-Free Internet Marketing Tactics to Establish Authority in Your Field and Promote Your Service-Based Business.*

- *From Entrepreneur to Infopreneur: Make Money with Books, eBooks and Information Products*

- *LEAP! 101 Ways to Grow Your Business*

Stephanie is also founder and CEO of the Nonfiction Authors Association, a vibrant educational community for experienced and aspiring writers, and the Nonfiction Writers Conference, an annual event conducted entirely online. A frequent speaker at business events and on the radio, she has been featured in *Entrepreneur, BusinessWeek,* and *Wired* magazine.

See also:

- @steph__chandler and @NonfictionAssoc on Twitter
- Facebook.com/NonfictionAuthorsAssociation
- Facebook.com/AuthorStephanieChandler
- NonfictionAuthorsAssociation.com
- NonfictionWritersConference.com
- AuthorityPublishing.com
- StephanieChandler.com

I love to hear from readers! Please send me your feedback and your success stories as a result of reading this book: Stephanie@NonfictionAuthorsAssociation.com.

Karl W. Palachuk is a business owner, entrepreneur, speaker, author, and Small Business Consultant. He has owned several successful businesses, primarily in the fields of technical consulting and book publishing. As a trainer and coach Karl has worked with thousands of business owners and managers to help them create and implement successful business models.

This is Karl's ninth book. All of his books are non-fiction and most were written for computer consultants. One exception is *Relax Focus Succeed: A Guide To Balancing Your Personal And Professional Lives And Being More Successful In Both.* Relax Focus Succeed® is Karl's framework for balancing your life and finding success in all areas of your life (work, home, romance, parenthood, etc.).

Karl has been a featured speaker at conferences and seminars over the last fifteen years. He is a Microsoft Certified Systems Engineer with a Bachelor's Degree from Gonzaga University and a Master's Degree from The University of Michigan. He is also a Microsoft Small Business Specialist, and has been on advisory panels for a variety of companies and professional organizations.

IF YOU LIKE THIS BOOK, YOU'LL LOVE THE NONFICTION AUTHORS ASSOCIATION!

MEMBER BENEFITS INCLUDE:

- Weekly educational teleseminars and past event recordings
- Exclusive content added weekly (Templates, Checklists, Worksheets)
- Access to our active members-only communities on Facebook and LinkedIn
- Marketing "Homework" (quick tips) sent weekly via email
- Complimentary admission to any NFAA local chapter meeting across the US and Canada
- Meet the Members program: Share your book announcements via our monthly email and get featured in our blog and social media networks, reaching over 100k people
- Discounts with NFAA partners: IngramSpark, Office Depot, PR Newswire, ProfNet, and more
- Discounted registration for the Nonfiction Book Awards, Nonfiction Writers Conference, online courses and our exclusive Author Toolkits

JOIN THE NONFICTION AUTHORS ASSOCIATION!
NONFICTIONAUTHORSASSOCIATION.COM/JOIN

MEMBER FEEDBACK:

"**As a new author, I can't say enough good things about the wealth of information I've received from NFAA.** The worksheets and information on specific topics are simply excellent! **Thank you so much for the untold hours of research you've spared me** as well as helping me know what I didn't know I needed to know!"
Marcia Grace, *Calm, Creative, Joyful: Lessons in Transforming Your Life*, marciagrace.com

"I joined the Nonfiction Authors Assoc. about six months ago and **I can't say enough about how helpful all the info is that I receive weekly** on everything I need to know as an author. I have just finished a second book and **the info on finding agents, on self-publishing, and other valuable tips is extremely helpful.**"
– Sandra CH Smith, Author of *A Cook's Tour of Epicuria — One Woman's Adventures*

"I've been with NFAA since Stephanie started the group and feel that she has worked hard ever since to constantly increase the value she brings to members. As a longtime self-published author, I also believe she is **raising the standards of our whole industry by providing real value in educating nonfiction writers** about the professional way to go about creating and publishing content. I very much appreciate what she has done and continues to do for us all, and one of the best ways she does it is through the annual Nonfiction Writers Conference. She always has the best speakers, and last year when she stepped in for one who couldn't show up at the last minute (which happens to every conference everywhere and certainly doesn't reflect on her), I frankly thought it was one of the best sessions of the whole event and hope she won't wait for an AWOL presenter to do so again."
– Mary Shafer, Author/Publisher, Word Forge Books, *Metal Detecting For Beginners: 101 Things I Wish I'd Known When I Started*, Detecting101.com

"**I absolutely love all the resources the association offers**–the downloads, the teleseminar recordings and the amazing discounts. Though I've been an author for many years now, I still find all kinds of new tips and ideas through NFAA. **It's one of the best investments I've ever made in my author career!**"

– Donna Hartley, Author of the *Fire Up Your Life* series, DonnaHartley.com

"After an earlier career as a comedy writer (I wrote for *The Monkees* and *Love American Style*) I have become excited about nonfiction writing on some new breakthroughs I've discovered in my second career of Conflict Resolution. **I am grateful to NFAA for the tremendous support and guidance I have received** in making this transition. **NFAA is a great organization!**"

– David Evans, HelpUshealAmerica.com

"I consider it a privilege to be a member of the Nonfiction Authors Association. **The resources that are available to new and established authors are outstanding. The Nonfiction Writers Conference is always jam-packed with great sessions** and this year I was invited by one of the panel agents to submit a book proposal during Pitch the Literary Agents! As an up and coming author I find great value in the monthly teleseminars as well. **I would encourage anyone who desires to become an established nonfiction author to join the Nonfiction Authors Association–you'll be glad you did!**"

– Akua Carmichael, Author of *My Lifeprint*

"**NFAA helped me launch my first book into the world successfully**. The templates and information on the web site are things I could not find anywhere else. I cannot wait to attend my first conference."

– Alison Buehler, Author of *Rethinking Women's Health*

JOIN THE NONFICTION AUTHORS ASSOCIATION!
NONFICTIONAUTHORSASSOCIATION.COM/JOIN

CPSIA information can be obtained
at www.ICGtesting.com
Printed in the USA
LVHW040050240419
615328LV00036B/927/P